The
LLANDUDNO &
COLWYN BAY
ELECTRIC RAILWAY

by
Keith Turner

THE OAKWOOD PRESS

© Oakwood Press 1993

ISBN 0 85361 450 4

Typeset by Gem Publishing Company, Brightwell, Wallingford, Oxfordshire.

Printed by Alpha Print (Oxon) Ltd, Crawley Mill, Oxford.

Acknowledgements

This book would not have been made possible without the help of many people: the librarians and staff of Llandudno, Colwyn Bay and the University College of North Wales, Bangor libraries; the archivists and staff of the then Caernarvonshire and Denbighshire record offices; Lens of Sutton; Stuart Rivers and Peter Smith of the Llandudno Tramway Society and its successor, the Llandudno & Colwyn Bay Electric Railway Society; Su Swingle, Vic Bradley, Dudley Caton, John Manners, D. Trevor Rowe, D.W.K. Jones, Richard Albutt, Derek Chaplin, G. Burrows, John Gillham for much helpful additional detail, and especially Margaret Donnison – who also drew the maps. And to anyone who assisted in any way and has inadvertently been omitted from this list, my sincere apologies and thanks.

Further information regarding the LCBER Society can be obtained from the Membership Secretary at 12 Y Felin, Conwy, Gwynedd LL32 8LW.

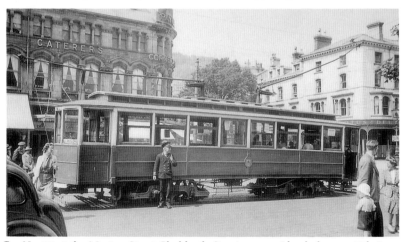

Car No. 17 at the Mostyn Street-Gloddaeth Street corner, Llandudno on 19th June, 1945. This is the original stock with Mountain and Gibson equal-wheeled bogies.

E.C. Haywood

Published by
The OAKWOOD PRESS
P.O.Box 122, Headington, Oxford.

A general view of the Promenade at Llandudno capturing the grandeur and elegance of the buildings   *Oakwood Collection*

Contents

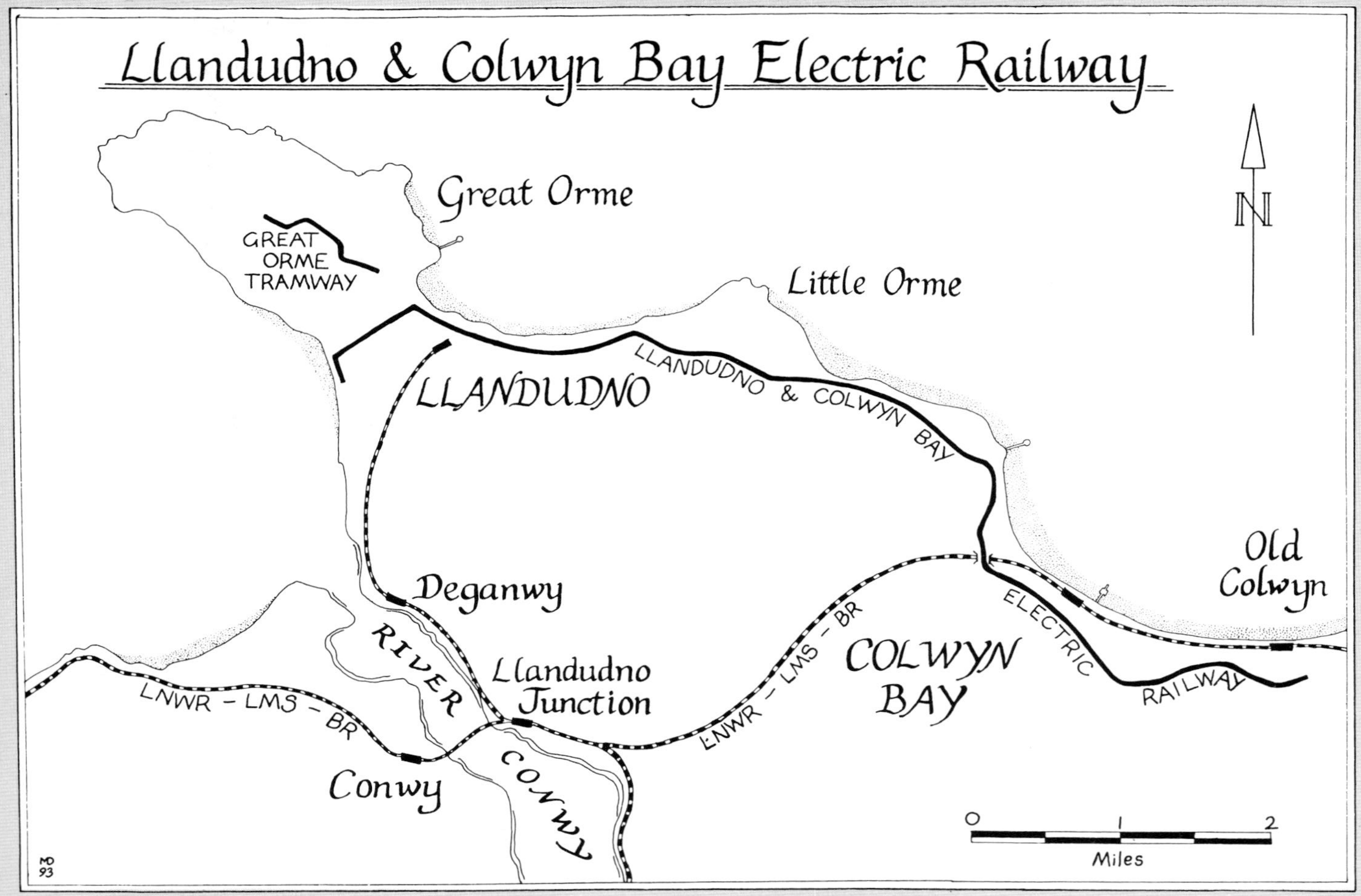

Llandudno & Colwyn Bay Electric Railway

N

Great Orme

Little Orme

GREAT ORME TRAMWAY

LLANDUDNO

LLANDUDNO & COLWYN BAY

Old Colwyn

ELECTRIC RAILWAY

COLWYN BAY

LNWR - LMS - BR

Deganwy

Llandudno Junction

RIVER CONWY

Conwy

LNWR - LMS - BR

Miles

2

1

0

A diagrammatic route map of the system

Introduction

North Wales was an area rich in tramway schemes but poor in actual lines. Of the few which were constructed, probably the most famous is the Great Orme Tramway, if only for the reason that it still operates today. The second most famous, and undoubtedly of more interest to the tramway enthusiast, was one that also served Llandudno: the Llandudno & Colwyn Bay Electric Railway. Despite its title it was a tramway, not a railway, and of all the North Wales tramways it had the longest route mileage, the largest car fleet and, at the outset, the greatest problems. How it overcame those, and what happened thereafter, is the subject matter of the following pages.

This account is based primarily on the relevant sections of the author's *North Wales Tramways*, published in 1979 but for several years now out of print. For this history the opportunity has been taken to expand the narrative at several points where further information has come to light, to increase greatly the number of photographic and other illustrations and, wherever relevant, to bring the story up to date.

No. 1 (ex-Accrington) descending the Little Orme towards Bodafon Fields in May 1951.   *D.W.K. Jones*

Rhos depot crew posing in front of car No. 24 in 1952. Only two crews were qualified to drive this vehicle (and No. 23) because of the Westinghouse air braking system and unusual controller.

H.L. Runnett

Chapter One
A Matter of Some Doubt

The early history of the Llandudno & Colwyn Bay Electric Railway is convoluted in the extreme and, if set out in full detail, would more than fill this book several times over. Much of the tramway's lengthy promotion story is, quite frankly, exceedingly boring – and has been so ever since it ceased to be of relevance to those directly concerned in the events of the dozen or so years spanning the turn of the century. What follows in this Chapter and the next is a potted version of the promotional aspirations, squabbles and set-backs that preceded the opening of the line; by presenting only the main and ultimately relevant events (and non-events!) it is hoped that a far clearer account of what took place during this period can be achieved.

As anyone who has visited the town will know, the most distinctive feature of Llandudno is the Great Orme; indeed, before the modern town was laid out it was about the *only* distinctive feature of the area. From the west, as far along the coast as Bangor, it appears to be an off-shore island rising abruptly from the sea; it is in fact a limestone mass some two miles long and one mile wide with steep cliffs on three sides but on the fourth – the southern side – it is connected by a very low, very flat strip of land to the rest of the mainland. St Tudno's church on the comparatively level summit gave its name to the parish (Llandudno in Welsh meaning the church of Tudno) and originally served the few miners' cottages huddled together on the landward side. As late as the mid-19th century these and two small inns were the only habitations on the peninsula, then part of the estate of the Hon. E.M.L. Mostyn, MP.

By this date North Wales was already becoming 'tourist conscious' and Mostyn realised that the rise of the fashionable watering-place need by no means be confined to the south coast of England; with this in mind he began his grand scheme, not only to build from scratch a complete resort, but then to elevate it to a position in the north equal to that held by Brighton in the south. Accordingly, in 1849, he offered and sold 176 plots of land on the low-lying peninsula; the scheme had taken its first steps towards becoming an unqualified success fulfilling all of Mostyn's hopes.

So sprang up the town that exists today, facing out to the north-east across the sands of Ormes Bay with the Great Orme on the left and its smaller namesake to the east, the Little Orme, on the right. With its broad promenade and majestic sweep of hotels and boarding houses along the bay it followed rigidly the pattern of its day, but in one important respect it was unique – and that one respect was without doubt one of the principal reasons behind Llandudno's success: behind the town was *another* beach – a longer, wider, more desolate stretch of sand bordering the Conwy estuary. This added attraction (and the splendid views from it), together with the impressive majesty of the Great Orme, meant that the project could hardly fail. In 1881 its population was 4,193 and by 1891 it had grown by nearly half as much again to 6,065; ten years later it had become an Urban District (principally by absorbing its neighbouring Civil Parish of Eglwys Rhos) with

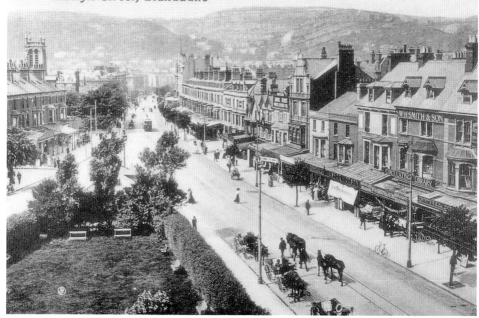

Pre-World War I commercial postcard view of the then single track tramway in Mostyn Street and Mostyn Broadway, Llandudno, with one of the 1909 single-deckers in the distance and beyond that the Great Orme – a scene surprisingly little-changed today. *Author's Collection*

An early commercial postcard view of an original single-decker in Conway Road, Colwyn Bay, when the line was still single-tracked. *Author's Collection*

a total of 9,279 inhabitants (a figure which could probably be safely doubled – or even tripled – anytime during the summer months). So Llandudno has grown to this day, to twice the 1901 figure: purely residential, relying completely and utterly on its annual surfeit of holiday-makers and conference-goers to the total exclusion of any other form of industry (apart from the necessary services needed to cater for inhabitants and visitors alike).

Less than five miles along the coast to the south-east, past the Little Orme, the township of Colwyn Bay experienced a similar boom in the wake of Llandudno's ascension. A century ago the town was virtually non-existent; what settlement there was in the area was centred around the villages of (Old) Colwyn, a short distance inland to the east, and Llandrillo-yn-Rhos, similarly situated to the west. By 1887 though it had developed sufficiently as a resort in Llandudno's wake to warrant being placed under a Local Board as a local government area in its own right; the 1891 census returned a population of 4,754 and four years later the Colwyn Bay & Colwyn Urban District Council was incorporated. In 1901 the population was not far behind that of Llandudno at 8,689 and the town was growing rapidly, swallowing up as suburbs Old Colwyn, Llandrillo-yn-Rhos and the inhabited headland to the west between Colwyn and the Little Orme known as Rhos-on-Sea.

Contemporary with the promotion of the Great Orme Tramway in Llandudno in the 1880s and 1890s as part tourist amenity, part local transport service, was the idea of linking that town with Colwyn Bay by a direct tramway or light railway. The London & North Western Railway provided only a rather roundabout route between them via the Llandudno branch line (opened 1858) to Llandudno Junction and thence along the main Chester–Holyhead line (opened 1848) to Colwyn Bay. A more direct route would also have had the advantage of passing through the principal built-up areas avoided by the railway, thus tapping potential traffic at source. This idea was first mooted during the early 1890s, gaining momentum as a result of the 1896 Light Railways Act which made the whole process of obtaining the necessary authorisation considerably cheaper than previously had been the case.

Things now started to move quickly: interested local parties, headed by George Griffiths, applied in December 1896 for a Light Railway Order to construct 4½ miles of 3 ft 6 in. gauge electric tramway between the towns at an estimated cost of over £28,000; the application, heard at Colwyn Bay on 23rd February, 1897, was rejected on the grounds that the interests of the local landowners and Llandudno Corporation had not been sufficiently considered.

Undaunted by this setback, the promoters made their next move on 9th May of the same year when the Light Railway & General Construction Co. Ltd (LR&GCCo.) was registered, to construct the proposed line, with a nominal capital of 75,000 Ordinary shares and an equal number of 6 per cent Cumulative Preference shares. The four Directors were J. Eckersley, D.R. Gibb, E. Hewitt and T.H. Fitzsimmons; the Secretary was John Morris and the registered office in Manchester. At the same time the company applied to the Light Railway Commissioners for the necessary Light Railway Order, the Directors and proprietors meeting to approve the draft order on 30th August. The application this time was for authorisation for a much grander scheme of 8 miles 25.45 chains of light railway, as one line, from the eastern end of Bay View Road at the corner of Greenfield Road in Colwyn Bay, over Penrhyn Hill (the landward side of the Little Orme), through Llandudno town centre and thence southwards to Deganwy railway station on the LNWR's Llandudno branch at the mouth of the Conwy estuary. The gauge proposed was still 3 ft 6 in., the tramway to be worked by animal power (i.e. horse) or electricity. The estimated cost for this longer line was just over £65,000.

The public enquiry into the application was held by the Commissioners in Colwyn Bay on 12th November, 1897; their decision was deferred until a second sitting on 18th May, 1898 on account of the declared opposition of Llandudno UDC. The latter had made an application for a Board of Trade Provisional Tramway Order to construct part of the proposed line (2 miles 65 chains) itself; in April 1898 however the UDC dropped its own scheme in favour of the company's. The Commissioners decided in favour of the LR&GCCo. and their approval was confirmed on 2nd June, 1899 by the Board of Trade in the shape of the Llandudno & Colwyn Bay Light Railway Order, 1898.

In addition to the above-mentioned proposals, the following points are especially important since this Order provided the basis for the subsequent eventual construction of the tramway: three years were allowed for the compulsory purchase of the land needed and for the completion of the works; electric traction was permitted and, under Section 76 of the Order, the sum of £2,980 had to be paid into court by the company before it could exercise its powers. (Section 77 provided for the repayment of this deposit when the line was opened.) Powers for compulsory purchase of the concern were given to the three local authorities involved: after 28 years for Llandudno UDC and after 25 years for Colwyn Bay UDC and Conway RDC.

This initial flurry of activity over, the scheme entered a new phase of procrastination, promises and pleading that lasted five years before anything concrete was achieved. At the bottom of it all was a simple matter of time and money – or, more correctly, a lack of those two commodities. Legal and other costs had amounted to £17,000 by the end of 1899; two years later that sum had risen to £25,000, by which time the company's registered office had moved to Bush House, Bush Lane, London EC. As the raising of the capital proved a slower process than had been originally envisaged, so the company was forced to spend money in purchasing time extensions just to retain its powers. Nor was the situation helped by the attitude of those who were in a position to speed up the proceedings. As the *Caernarvon & Denbigh Herald* of 23rd August, 1901 declared in a leader article:

> The petulant obstruction, the policy of opposition by the council, the exorbitant demands of Lord Mostyn, and the thousand and one claims made by adjacent local authorities nearly defeated the promotion of the movement by piling on heavy floating expenditure.

Continued on page 26

LIGHT RAILWAYS ACT, 1896.

LLANDUDNO AND COLWYN BAY LIGHT RAILWAY ORDER, 1898.

ORDER

MADE BY THE

LIGHT RAILWAY COMMISSIONERS,

AND MODIFIED AND CONFIRMED BY THE

BOARD OF TRADE,

AUTHORISING THE CONSTRUCTION OF

LIGHT RAILWAYS FROM COLWYN BAY TO LLANDUDNO IN
THE COUNTIES OF DENBIGH AND CARNARVON.

Presented to both Houses of Parliament by Command of Her Majesty.

LONDON:
PRINTED FOR HER MAJESTY'S STATIONERY OFFICE,
By DARLING & SON, Ltd., 1-3, Great St. Thomas Apostle, E.C.

And to be purchased, either directly or through any Bookseller, from
EYRE & SPOTTISWOODE, East Harding Street, Fleet Street, E.C., and
32, Abingdon Street, Westminster, S.W.; or
JOHN MENZIES & Co., 12, Hanover Street, Edinburgh, and
90, West Nile Street, Glasgow; or
HODGES, FIGGIS, & Co., Limited, 104, Grafton Street, Dublin.

1899.

[C. 9395.]   *Price 3d.*

Title page of the 1898 Light Railway Order.

The tramway as first laid in Gloddaeth Street, Llandudno. This view is looking towards the West Shore; here side poles gave way to span wires to support the overhead. This and the following construction photographs were captured on film for Bruce Peebles in early 1907

The spacious Gloddaeth Street, looking east towards Hooson's Corner.

Looking back towards Hooson's Corner from Mostyn Street.

Mostyn Broadway, looking east, with the Grand Theatre in the mid-distance and the Little Orme beyond. Note the still relatively ... of thi ... end of the town.

Courtesy N.B. Traction Collection

The track crossing Bodafon Fields, looking east from the Llandudno end.

Bodafon Fields with the track still under construction, looking back towards Llandudno with the sweep of the bay visible on the right.
Courtesy N.B. Traction Collection

Bryn-y-Bia Road with the overhead now supported by side poles.

The major cutting just over the crest of Penrhyn Hill at Penrhynside, shortly after the tramway's construction.

Courtesy N.B. Traction Collection

Erecting the overhead, slightly further down Penrhyn Hill.

Marine Drive shortly after track had been laid. Note the lattice poles on this section.

Near the site of the car shed just before its erection, with an unusual unidentified contractor's locomotive at work.

Courtesy N.B. Traction Collection

Car No. 3 on Penrhyn Hill during a trial run for the contractors.

Courtesy N.B. Traction Collection

Another view of No. 3 at the same location.

Under the 1898 Order the date for completion was 2nd June, 1902; with nothing at all begun the company – now entitled the Llandudno, Colwyn Bay, and Rhyl [!] Electric Traction Co. Ltd (LCB&RETCo.) – applied in November 1901 for an extension of time. The Light Railway Commissioners held their enquiry in Colwyn Bay on 5th March, 1902 and approved both this application and one for a 52.75-chain deviation within Colwyn Bay. This provided a different route from Rhos-on-Sea up Rhos Road and across the fields, skirting rather than crossing the estate of Sir George Cayley (who had unsuccessfully opposed this portion of the authorised route in 1898), before rejoining the 1898 route over the LNWR main line and down Princes Road, passing close to the railway station before terminating at the eastern end of Bay View Road. In June, while awaiting the Board of Trade's confirmation of the Order, the company finally paid into court the £2,980 specified in Section 76 of the 1898 Order. This meant that the company was only now in a position to carry out its undertaking – with no time left to start, let alone finish the work!

Not until 26th September, when the Board of Trade confirmed the Llandudno & Colwyn Bay Light Railway (Deviation and Amendment) Order, 1903, was the LCB&RETCo. officially granted extra time: the three-year time period for the purchase of land was increased to four years and six months and that for the completion of the works to five years, both dates to be calculated from 2nd June, 1899,

> Provided that if the actual construction of the railway of 1898 be not substantially commenced by the thirtieth day of September 1903 the powers of the Company under the Order of 1898 and this Order shall cease.

The last section of track to be doubled (1928–9) was between the Brompton Avenue railway bridge and the then terminus in Colwyn Bay (at the same time as the road was being widened by the UDC).   *Courtesy LCBER Society*

A further proviso was that Rhos Road could not be used by trams until that section of the highway occupied by the light railway had been widened, in accordance with an agreement dated 15th December, 1902 with Cayley. Presumably this work was never done as the section of the route was later altered (because of the expense involved in the widening?); it appears though that the land for the line between Rhos-on-Sea and the West Parade, Llandudno, was all purchased within the new time limit. The route onwards from Rhos through Colwyn Bay was not regarded as a satisfactory one and alternative plans were drawn up. As for the promise to investors included in the company's title of reaching Rhyl – indeed, it had hopes of reaching Prestatyn further to the east – no attempts were ever made to obtain powers for such a line and, as will be seen below, the promise quickly evaporated. Furthermore, the company was hampered by another proviso in the Order preventing it carrying out road works in Llandudno and Colwyn Bay urban districts during the months of June to September, i.e. the holiday season.

The LCB&RET Co. was now in something of a sorry state. Only 11,560 shares had been issued, of which Thomas S. Turnbull, the company's one Director, held 1,000. Of the remaining £10,560 subscribed capital, 9,530 shares were held by the Welsh Electric Traction Co. Ltd – another company with a Manchester registered office of which Morris was also the Secretary. But – in refutation of a statement made by the company's solicitor in March 1902 that 'the company had done no work, nor purchased a yard of land, and that practically all the money had been spent' – things were now about to happen.

During the 1928–9 Conway Road track-doubling the tracks between the junctions with Coed Pella Road and Woodland Road were interlaced. This view shows the work being done. *Courtesy LCBER Society*

1920s track-doubling work in progress by Rhos Promenade.   *Courtesy LCBER Society*

A very weather-beaten No. 17 of 1909 heads towards Colwyn Bay along Rhos Promenade, pursued by No. 12 of 1907, sometime during the 1920s.

Courtesy LCBER Society

Chapter Two
Open at Last

On 10th October, 1903 the *North Wales Chronicle* announced that work on the tramway was at long last underway: at the end of September a start had been made near Rhos on a reserved section some 1,000 yards long. A total of 33 men were engaged in filling-in and raising the route of the trackbed to the required level, erecting fences and laying sleepers. Stone for the work was obtained from a nearby quarry – nine men and eight carts were reported to be occupied in this work. From certain other contemporary events it is clear that this move to begin construction was merely a political one: Llandudno UDC was again preparing to apply for a Board of Trade (BoT) Order to build its own tramway in Llandudno and the town's Surveyor had already been instructed to modify the 1897 plans accordingly. Furthermore, on 26th September Cayley had written to the UDC requesting that the Council join him in petitioning the BoT to stop the progress of the tramway: he claimed that the work done was not sufficient to be deemed 'a substantial commencement' under the terms of the 1903 Order. It was, in short, a very lightly laid line to serve Mr W. Horton's brick works!

The LCB&RETCo. continued its customary policy of uttering reassuring noises at every opportunity. Mr W.G. Rhodes of Messrs Hewitt & Rhodes of Manchester, the engineers retained for the construction, had a meeting with the UDC and confidently stated that 'although he did not anticipate that the railway would be in full working order till Whitsuntide next', he thought that parts of it might be. Towards the end of October the Council Surveyor inspected the work done and reported that 44 men were engaged upon it and that 250 yards or so of track had been well laid – some previously condemned sleepers having been replaced!

At the beginning of November the Surveyor again visited the site and reported that the trackbed had been prepared for a distance of 800 yards, 70 men were now employed and large quantities of rails and sleepers had been delivered. Horton was now financing the work and all in all it seemed as if the tramway was fast becoming fact. By January 1904 Rhos Road had been reached and crossed for Colwyn Bay UDC received complaints about the tramway track there – the rails were supposed to lie flush with the road surface but had instead been laid 'on sleepers with shingle from the beach' heaped around them.

On 10th March, 1904 the *Tramway and Railway World* happily announced that Messrs Hewitt & Rhodes had secured the contract (which was worth £99,440) with the company – now entitled the Llandudno & Colwyn Bay Electric Traction Co. Ltd (L&CBETCo.) – for the construction of the line from Mostyn Street, Llandudno, to Rhos-on-Sea. It was to be completed by 1st May and, according to that journal, 1½ miles had already been laid whilst work on a new contract was being commenced by sub-contractors. The truth was sadly different. At the beginning of June the company applied to the BoT for another year's extension, the existing deadline expiring on the second day of that month. Track laid equalled just 365 yards.

Lieut-Col P.G. von Donop, RE, of the BoT heard the company's application for a further time extension on Friday 15th July, 1904 in the Colwyn Bay Hotel. Reporting on the meeting, the *Chronicle* of 23rd July stated that only two men (!) were engaged on building the line. According to the newspaper account, it was stated that the contract for the line had in fact been placed on 25th April with the Welsh Electric Traction Co. Ltd ('laughter'): 'The contract would be sublet for the construction because the company was not a constructing company (laughter)'. Apparently £40,000 of fresh financial backing was to be provided by a London group, the Tramways Extension Syndicate, and this induced the BoT to grant a time extension until 23rd February, 1905 with the possibility of a further six months to complete and open the line if the work was progressing satisfactorily. The construction contract was due to expire on 1st May, 1905.

It must have come as no surprise to anyone when 1st May, 1905 came and went without any further work having been done on the tramway. The story now takes on a familiar ring as the promoters continued to spend what capital they could raise on raising more capital and arranging time extensions to buy more time to raise more capital to buy more time . . . and all the while the local councils grew more and more irate on the outside of this vicious circle. Then in 1906 the circle broke when the L&CBETCo. went into liquidation; as a stop-gap measure to salvage the company's powers a nominal company, the Caernarvonshire Electric Traction Syndicate Ltd (CETS), was formed until a new start could be made. This came on 25th July, 1906 with the registration of the Llandudno & District Electric Tramway Construction Co. Ltd (L&DETC), set up to adopt agreements with the L&CBETCo. (which it absorbed on 23rd August), the CETS and the old-established (and experienced in tramway construction) Edinburgh firm of Bruce Peebles & Co. Ltd to take over the necessary powers, issue contracts for the work and equipment, complete and actually operate the line. One wonders just what the local residents expected to come of it all!

This time though the move was destined to succeed. The L&DETCCo. got off to a good start from the very beginning: almost all its 1,000 £100 shares were immediately issued, no doubt helped by the fact that Bruce Peebles guaranteed a 6 per cent dividend on them until 30th June, 1907. A. Belton Macartney was appointed as the first Company Secretary and the registered office was set up in London at 13, St Helens Place, EC; the four Directors – Stephen Sellon, MICE (Chairman), Thomas Stoker, Roland S. Portheim and R.A. Freemantle, MIEE – promptly placed the construction contract with Bruce Peebles. This Board had strong connections with other tramway and electric power companies, both at home and abroad, and Portheim was Bruce Peebles' Managing Director so it was hardly surprising that work pushed ahead on preparing the trackbed; early in 1907 tracklaying recommenced. In January two cars were brought to the site for trials on the line; these had originally been built for another Bruce Peebles' contract (Canvey Island) but had since been returned to the manufacturer. (Further details of these cars are given in Chapter 10.)

In startling contrast to the on-off-on efforts of the previous years,

Car No. 23, on the front at Rhos on Sea in 1952.   *H.L. Runnett*

Service car No. 5 (ex-Accrington) on 21st May, 1951 in the Gloddaeth Street loop passing toastrack 21 working a Special for members of the Light Railway Transport League.   *D.W.K. Jones*

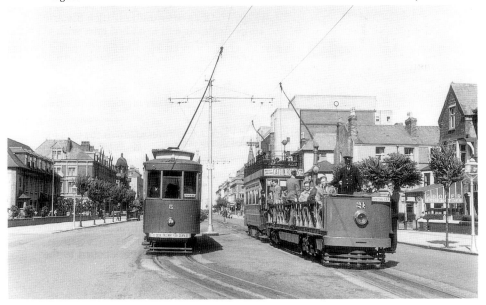

construction went forward at what must have seemed an incredible rate. It had to: the latest time extension granted was only until 21st November of that year. Under the supervision of Bruce Peebles' engineer, Mr W.C. Waite, and his assistant engineer, Mr E. Scholfield, the trackbed had been blasted out over the lower slopes of the Little Orme at Penrhynside, track laid and wiring erected. Within a matter of months a single line (with passing loops being added) stretched from the depot at Rhos-on-Sea to the West Shore, Llandudno and the full dual overhead wiring was in place. Grooved tramway rails weighing 90 lb. per yard were used throughout, spiked to wooden sleepers and ballasted on the reserved sections and laid on 18 in. wide by 9 in. deep concrete foundations on the roadway stretches where they were paved with wood blocks. In the centre of Llandudno the blocks were covered with tar macadam in an attempt to reduce noise levels. The use of tramway (rather than railway) rails on the more rural sections was because the company anticipated those portions of the right-of-way would soon be converted into roads; indeed, alongside parts of the line building plots were now being sold as a direct spin-off from the tramway's coming. The overhead wires were supported by a mixture of bracket arms and span wires with tubular poles throughout (except on some straight rural stretches where lattice-girder poles were used). Current at 500–550 volts DC was supplied by Llandudno UDC from its power station in Maesdu Road which had opened on 5th November, 1898 equipped with an Allen steam engine and an eight-pole 300 kW generator supplied by Bruce Peebles. Distribution cables were by Callender's Cable & Construction Co.

Arrangements for working the line were not neglected. A fleet of 14 single-deck cars was ordered from the Midland Railway Carriage & Wagon Co. Ltd, Mr W.H. Moorhouse (of tramway experience at Tynemouth and Barnsley) was appointed General Manager, Sellon (formerly a member of the Board of Trade Committee on Light Railways and Engineer to the British Electric Traction Co. Ltd) was appointed Chief Engineer and a staff of men with at least two years' tramway experience each recruited. On Friday 9th August the first trial trips were run over the line and, according to the *Electrical Review* of the following week,

> The cars ran satisfactorily, but it is stated that the B. of T. will not grant the necessary certificate to carry passengers until the cars are provided with hand-brakes in addition to the Westinghouse brakes.

This modification – if not already in hand – was soon made to the cars for on 26th September Lieut-Col von Donop inspected the completed five miles of line between the West Shore and Rhos-on-Sea on behalf of the BoT and found them basically satisfactory; the opening was set for October. On Thursday 17th of that month the first passenger-carrying trips were made by the new cars, though the occasion was a private one for the benefit of the company officials and guests. With those making the trip over the line were a party of LNWR officials, Messrs Waite and Scholfield of Bruce Peebles and Messrs G.W. Stevenson and A.W. Thomas of the car builders.

Two days later, on Saturday 19th October, 1907, the line opened to the general public with cars starting simultaneously from both ends. (The first car from the Llandudno end is believed to have been No. 14 whilst the identity of the other has been lost.) During the afternoon and evening two more cars were brought into service to cope with the traffic. The opening was in keeping with the history of the project: no ceremony (other than cheers and bell-ringing from spectators), a limited half-hourly service and No. 11 sticking on Penrhyn Hill. Nevertheless 4,434 passenger journeys were made that day and over £45 taken in receipts. The first ticket issued was purchased by Councillor J. McMaster of Llandudno UDC Lighting Committee.

Another view of the track-doubling work in Conway Road, looking towards the interlaced section. *Courtesy LCBER Society*

A misty day in November 1955 with an open-topper about to ascend Penrhyn Hill, as seen from the upper deck of a sister car. *D.W.K. Jones*

Penrhynside, seen on 9th June, 1938 from the top deck of an ex-Bournemouth car. *D.W.K. Jones*

"THE CRESCENT"

Boarding Establishment,
—— NEVILLE CRESCENT. ——

Charmingly situated on the Sea Front;
with views embracing the Great and
Little Ormes and the Carnarvonshire
range of mountains.
A few minutes' walk from the Pier,
Pavilion, Railway Station and Trams.
Private Tennis Lawn. Excellent Cuisine.
Table d'Hote 6.30.

TERMS MODERATE.

Mr. & Miss MORAN. Telegrams:
"Crescent Hotel,"
No. 9.

"RISBORO"

Boarding Residence,

Clement Avenue (near *Gloddaeth Street*).

LLANDUDNO.

From 5 - per day.

Is most conveniently and pleasantly situated, Facing
South, with magnificent views of the Welsh mountains,
and is only two or three minutes' walk from Pier, Pavilion,
Golf Links, and all the chief places of Amusement.
Trams pass near the house.

Excellent Cuisine. **S. F. COOPER, Proprietor.**
No. 12.

Establishments close to the route of the tramway were not loathe to announce that
they could be reached by the new line, as these two advertisements from the *Official
Guide to Llandudno* (c.1913) show.

The car shed soon after erection showing the original fleet inside.

Tramway Avenue from the depot, looking towards Rhos.

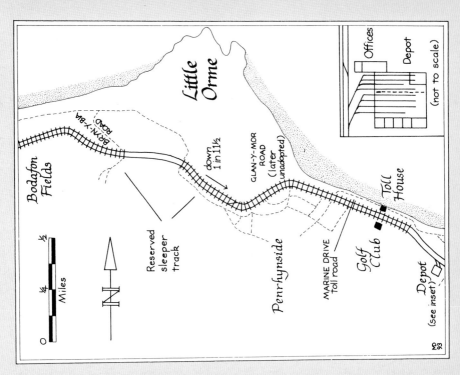

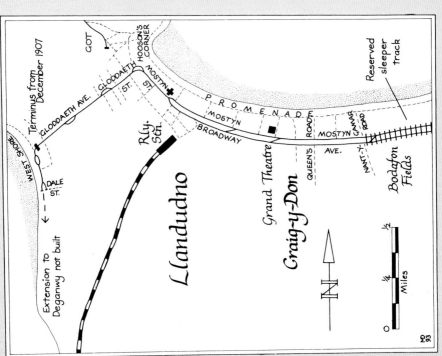

LCBER: Llandudno – Rhos Depot showing track alterations and final doubling.

Chapter Three
The Route Described

Finding a suitable point in the narrative at which to describe the tramway's route in detail is not an easy task for the simple reason that the details kept changing throughout the tramway's life. It will however be attempted here, with references included to future alterations – these will also be covered in later Chapters at the appropriate chronological points.

Prior to 1922 the western end of the LCBER was officially on the actual West Parade itself, opposite the end of Dale Street. Two short roads were provided at the terminus and a short passing loop was sited some 200 hundred yards or so down the line, just before it turned sharply right into Gloddaeth Avenue; otherwise this section was always single track. From 1922 onwards the official terminus was here, at the end of Gloddaeth Avenue, the 440 yards of track back round the corner and along to Dale Street being lifted that year (see Chapter 5). In actuality, this section had been abandoned shortly after the line opened and it was derelict by the start of World War I, a sand-swept reminder of the company's erstwhile dreams of reaching Deganwy.

From the West Shore the line ran straight across the Great Orme isthmus down Gloddaeth Avenue (where there was a passing loop for a while) and its extension Gloddaeth Street (another loop was sited here) before it swung abruptly right at Hooson's Corner into Mostyn Street. From 1909 a passing loop existed on the actual corner – a corner that gave rise to continual complaints about the squealing of trams as they rounded it (see Chapter 4). From here the single line ran down Mostyn Street for ¼ mile until it reached a point flanked by the Library and St John's Church where it doubled. (It should be borne in mind that in the first instance the line was laid entirely as a single one, with passing loops added as and when it was felt they were needed.) The double tracks carried on through to the first Colwyn Bay terminus, the work of doubling the line having been completed in a number of stages by that date.

Leaving Mostyn Street the double tracks entered that road's continuation, Mostyn Broadway, passing (on the right) the North Western Hotel and (on the left) what was later to be the Crosville bus depot and the Grand Theatre. Halfway between the North Western and the Grand was a trailing crossover and in 1953 another was laid outside the theatre. Still sweeping along the main thoroughfare of Llandudno, the tramway passed into Mostyn Avenue and left the town centre for the outlying district of Craig-y-Don, carrying on beyond the end of the highway into its first reserved section at the trailing crossover at Nant-y-Gamar Road.

The line now ran through Bodafon fields for ¾ mile, rising ever-steeper up the lower slopes of the Little Orme above Llandudno Bay. Reaching Bryn-y-Bia Road the tracks followed the side of the roadway for another ¼ mile to the summit of Penrhyn Hill – as this part of the Little Orme is known – at Penrhynside. Here began the 1 in 11½ miles descent (the line's steepest) on reserved track above and to the left of the main Llandudno–Colwyn Bay

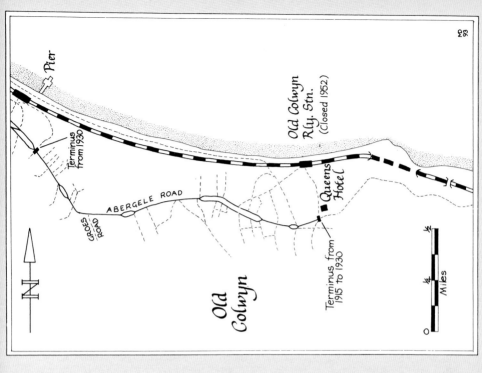

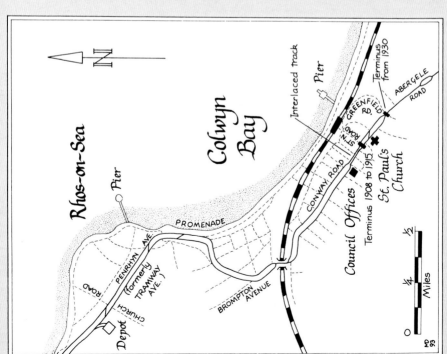

LCBER: Rhos Depot – Old Colwyn showing track alterations and final doubling

road which had been crossed at the summit; and so down the hill, along the reserved section that was later to become part of Glan-y-Mor Road and onto the open, sea-threatened Marine Drive toll road beside Penrhyn Bay. Here the Golf Clubhouse was passed on the right and the Toll House on the left before the line swung inland into Rhos-on-Sea down Penrhyn Avenue, reaching the depot and offices of the LCBER on the right just before another trailing crossover at the junction of the avenue and Church Road.

The tramway depot was situated on the landward side of the line and was connected to the Llandudno-bound track by two trailing points; the spur from each point led to four shed roads into the depot which had room for 20 cars. As well as housing the trams at night, this was where all minor repairs, overhauls and repainting jobs were done. Also housed here were the various staff and general offices, the latter having a frontage on the roadway next to the depot. A good indication of the strong rural character of much of the line when constructed is given by the fact that this now populous district was known, when the tramway arrived, as Klondyke on account of its isolation!

The end of Penrhyn Avenue – or Tramway Avenue, as it was formerly known – was reached ½ mile beyond the depot; immediately before this (until 1935) a trailing crossover existed at Colwyn Crescent. At the end of the avenue the line curved right, in the centre of Rhos, to emerge onto the Promenade which it occupied for ¼ mile. Turning inland once again, the tramway then passed through the residential area on the border of Rhos and Colwyn Bay before crossing the LNWR's main Chester–Holyhead railway line at Brompton Avenue bridge and joining Colwyn Bay's principal thoroughfare, Conway Road (now the A55). As the double tracks of the tramway reached the actual railway bridge they were briefly singled for it never proved possible to double the line here.

For the remaining mile along Conway Road and its continuation, Abergele Road, the track was again double, though for a 200-yard stretch between the Council Offices and the top of Station Road the two tracks were interlaced on account of the narrowness of the roadway. Halfway between Station Road and the terminus, outside St Paul's Church, was the line's final trailing crossover. This was not the tramway's terminus throughout its life however for between the years 1915 and 1930 it extended for another mile as a single-track line, with three passing loops and a short double-track section, along Abergele Road (the A55) to Old Colwyn, terminating by the Queens Hotel. The story of the opening and closing of this portion of the LCBER is told in the next two Chapters.

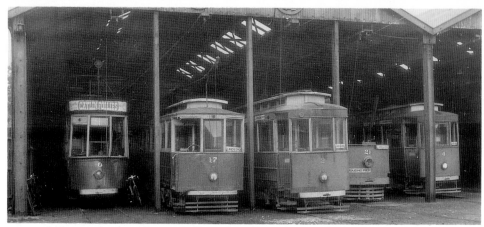

An impressive depot line-up in November 1955 with original cars Nos. 17 (ex-14) and 21, and second-hand cars Nos. 2, 4 and 9.   *D.W.K. Jones*

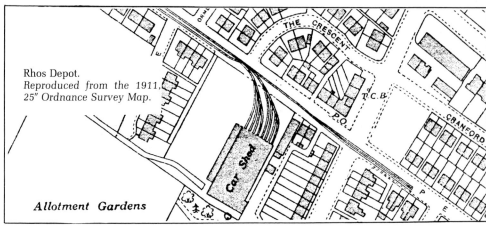

Rhos Depot.
*Reproduced from the 1911,
25" Ordnance Survey Map.*

A 1951 depot line-up with (*from left to right*) No. 18 (formerly No. 11 of 1907), No. 6 (ex-Bournemouth) and No. 24 (ex-Darwen).   *D.W.K. Jones*

Car No. 11 (ex-Bournemouth) at Penrhynside on 7th September, 1955.

Peter Johnson Collection

A timeless view of Bodafon Fields with two open-toppers about to pass. The Little
Orme is in the distance. *D.W.K. Jones*

Looking back along Tramway Avenue in the 1920s, from the cricket ground to the depot, with the Little Orme in the distance. From here to the Colwyn Bay terminus the line ran through a built-up area. *Courtesy LCBER Society*

Looking towards Rhos Depot during the 1920s along what is now Penrhyn Avenue, the builders' boards in the fields presaging later development. Note the lattice overhead masts used from Glan-y-Mor Road to the end of Tramway Avenue, later replaced by tubular posts (except in Glan-y-Mor Road). *Courtesy LCBER Society*

Cars Nos. 1 and 14 at Mostyn Street in August 1955.   *John Edgington*

Car No. 23 entering Colwyn Bay in June 1952.   *H.L. Runnett*

Looking up Gloddaeth Avenue, Llandudno, during the 1920s with a single-decker leaving the West Shore Terminus.   *Courtesy LCBER Society*

Gloddaeth Avenue, looking towards the North Shore during the 1920s.
                    Courtesy LCBER Society

Chapter Four

Expansion . . .

Full scheduled services were instituted in November 1907 from Rhos to the Llandudno terminus, but were modified the following month so that all cars terminated in Gloddaeth Avenue instead of proceeding through to the West Shore. This arrangement was stated by the company to give a quicker service with resulting benefits to the public; the cars would recommence going through to Dale Street in the summer when traffic warranted it (though they never, in fact, did). Authority to construct the extension from here across the sand dunes and the golf links to Deganwy was allowed to expire, one reason being that the hoped-for housing development (and hence potential traffic) had failed to materialise.

In November 1906 the L&DETCCo. had applied to the Light Railway Commissioners for another Light Railway Order to alter and extend the already authorised route of the tramway in Colwyn Bay. The Order, confirmed by the BoT on 30th September, 1907, was entitled the Llandudno and Colwyn Bay Light Railway (Extension and Amendment) Order, 1907 – a title that aptly summed up its contents. Under its provisions the former route planned for Colwyn Bay by the Orders of 1898 and 1903 was abandoned in favour of 2 miles 45.52 chains of new line from the bottom of Penrhyn Avenue at Rhos to a point in Abergele Road 202 yards east of Groes Road. This new route was the one eventually constructed (as described in the previous Chapter) though it was only about half the length the company wanted. A 19.42-chain loop from Conway Road down Penrhyn Road towards the station, then back up Station Road to Abergele Road, was included as a last attempt to reach the station but powers to construct this line were allowed to lapse.

Time allowed for completion of the works was extended under the Order to two years from 30th September for the new lines – though construction of the last 24 chains of the extension was not permitted to commence until the company had secured powers for a full extension to Old Colwyn. An extension time allowance of three years (from the same date) was given for the uncompleted portion of the 1898 tramway and 12 months were allowed for the company to widen Rhos Road to 42 feet, failing which £2,500 was to be paid for the local authority to do it; a further £3,000 was to be paid directly for two widenings in Abergele Road. The Order also postponed the local authority's compulsory purchase powers until six months after 2nd June, 1941 or every subsequent seven years.

Continuing its new, dynamic policy of actually getting things done, the company immediately commenced work on the Colwyn Bay section with an Easter 1908 date set for the opening. By March of that year construction was well under way and it seemed that the date would be met but completion of the final touches delayed the introduction of public services until 7th June. Total route mileage open was now 6 miles 48 chains, of which 1 mile 2 chains was double track, out of an authorised total of 8 miles 55 chains.

Now that it had at long last become a reality the tramway was handsomely meeting the expectations of its long-suffering supporters. The first general meeting of the L&DETCCo. had been held, under the chairmanship of Sellon, on 24th March, 1908 and receipts for 21 weeks (up to 13th March) of £1,542 announced – an average taking of over £72 per week throughout the non-tourist season; car miles were reported as 46,000 and the total number of passenger journeys 174,664. That the concern was proving a relatively prosperous one was of little doubt; 21st April, 1909 saw the company register a new, less cumbersome name – the Llandudno & Colwyn Bay Electrical Railway Ltd (LCBER). More tangible evidence of prosperity came later in the year when, in September, a further four single-deck cars were purchased as new (see Chapter 10 for details of these) from the United Electric Car Co. Ltd, bringing the stock total to an impressive eighteen. (During this year the loop referred to in Chapter 3 was laid at the corner of Mostyn Street and Gloddaeth Street as part of the provision of a better service programme.)

The fortunes of the LCBER had not escaped the notice of another company in the tramway world: Balfour, Beatty & Co. Ltd. This firm had been set up in 1909 by its joint managing directors, George Balfour and A.H. Beatty, to act as general and electrical engineers, contractors and operating managers for tramways, railways, lighting and power undertakings. In line with its policy of buying a sizeable interest in suitable concerns, such an interest was purchased in the LCBER Ltd and Balfour took a seat on the Board in 1910. (Apart from Balfour, Beatty & Co., he held directorships of fourteen other tramway and power concerns already and was a member of the council of the Tramways and Light Railways Association.)

In terms of public relations, by 1911 the honeymoon was over and the old familiar company–local authority antagonism was back again. This time it was to stay until the tramway closed nearly half a century later – and then even beyond that. While the line continued to develop, in this instance by doubling its track through Rhos, complaints began to be voiced concerning the state of the track elsewhere. The Colwyn Bay Surveyor was instructed by his Council to draw up a report on the condition of the line through the town so that representations could be made to the BoT; the company promised that the necessary repairs would be carried out by Easter. Complaints were also received from the public about the screeching of cars round the tight corner from Mostyn Street into Gloddaeth Street; assurances were given that this would be reduced by greasing the rails. (As mentioned earlier, the problem of noise at this corner dogged the tramway throughout its life and was never really solved. At a meeting of the Llandudno UDC in March 1911 the sound was referred to by one member as like 'the shrieks of Kilkenny cats'.) That same year, on the evening of 22nd June, 1911, two illuminated cars were run to celebrate the Coronation of King George V.

Moves to complete the extension to Old Colwyn were now coming to a head. Although the application for a Light Railway Order for the line had originally been made in May 1907 for a 1-mile extension along Abergele Road (estimated cost £5,870), the decision of the Light Railway Commissioners on this extension had been delayed all this time pending the outcome of a protracted dispute between the company and Colwyn Bay UDC over the necessary road widening which would be entailed. While the dispute dragged on a series of time extensions were successfully sought from the BoT for the last section of the line authorised under the 1907 Order; these were granted in 1909, 1910 and 1911, giving a final expiration date of 30th November, 1912.

In March 1911 the company put the blame for the delay on Colwyn Bay UDC, saying that an offer of £3,000 to cover the cost of the road widening had been refused and that other obstacles had been placed in the company's way. For its part the UDC denied this and stated that the sum offered was not sufficient to cover the costs involved – and besides, it was still owed £3,000 for road widening carried out under the 1907 Order! By October the UDC was seriously considering constructing the extension itself as it regarded the present terminus at the loop at the top of Station Road a dangerous one – especially since trams reputedly stood there illegally at night without displaying lights.

The matter was finally resolved by the Light Railway Commissioners with the granting of the Llandudno and Colwyn Bay Light Railway (Extension No. 2) Order, 1912, confirmed by the BoT on 1st August of that year, which authorised the construction of a 1 mile 6.22-chain extension down Abergele Road from the end of the 1907 authorised line to the junction with Queens Road. Three years were allowed for the completion of the line, during the construction of which the company was to widen Abergele Road to 24 ft wherever narrower than that (plus a footpath width of at least 6 ft). Construction of the extension was somewhat slow by the company's previous standards and the new line did not open until 26th March, 1915. (The work was delayed by the track-doubling programme which took priority; by the end of 1911 the double track had reached the eastern side of Penrhyn Hill and was within 50 yards of the loop at the summit.) Official total route mileage was now 8 miles 30 chains, the longest of the tramway's life. Of this, 5 miles 18 chains were now double track.

With respect to other company matters, this period saw J.E. Touche and C.H. Rigg join the Board and Freemantle leave (by 1908); Bruce Peebles' Director Andrew Wilson Tait join and Rigg and Portheim leave (by 1910); the moving of the registered office to Basildon House, Moorgate Street, London EC and the appointment (also by 1910) of A.W.R. Lovering as Secretary.

Brake adjustment before the descent!   *G.R. Thompson*

Service car No. 13 (ex-Bournemouth) in Gloddaeth Avenue alongside toastrack 21 on the 1951 Light Railway Transport League special.   *D.W.K. Jones*

Car No. 20 with a full load seen here at Penrhynside in August 1955.   *John Edgington*

Chapter Five
. . . and Contraction

With the eastern end of the line having reached a successful conclusion, it is time to travel back to the other terminus and investigate the state of affairs there. As described in the previous Chapter, the 1898 Order authorised the line to continue on from Llandudno to Deganwy; as already described however the tramway as constructed, after reaching the end of Gloddaeth Avenue at the West Shore, turned expectantly southwards along West Parade only to come to an abrupt halt – like the roadside itself – some 400 yards further on opposite the end of Dale Street. Like the rest of the line in Llandudno at that time, this section was single track, interrupted by a short loop at one end and the two-track terminus at the other. Powers to construct the Deganwy extension though had never been formally abandoned and time extensions had been granted along with those for other sections of the tramway. The truth was however that any passenger traffic between Llandudno and Deganwy would have been a very poor second in comparison with that between Llandudno and Colwyn Bay; there was in addition a direct railway link between the two places. Capital expenditure was therefore aimed in more profitable directions and once the extension to Old Colwyn was finished the line was regarded as complete. Powers to construct the Deganwy extension were accordingly permitted to lapse and in 1922 the West Parade section was officially abandoned, bringing the route mileage down to 8.14 miles (8 miles 10 chains).

The following table gives some basic details of the tramway's operations during the period leading up to World War I.

Year ending 30th November	Traffic receipts	Working expenditure	Passengers carried	Car miles
1907	£584	£2,959	63,931	13,380
1908	£12,068	£6,467	1,060,281	185,082
1909	£14,272	£10,001	1,356,323	247,843
1910	£14,725	£9,213	1,424,045	260,872
1911	£15,359	£8,001	1,505,603	267,141
1912	£16,199	£8,579	1,621,801	276,040
1913	£17,710	£8,395	1,768,142	272,908

The tramway now settled down to a fairly uneventful existence for the next dozen years or so, the first major happening being the purchase in 1920 of four open toastrack cars from English Electric (see Chapter 10), bringing the stock total to twenty-two. These cars were especially popular during the summer with visitors – though only when the weather was fine! The second occurrence of note took place two years later when, on Saturday 18th February, 1922, the tramway's employees went on strike in protest against the company's proposal, made on 15th February, to reduce their wages by 1s. (5p) per week on top of the statutory reduction of 3s. (15p) from 1st February imposed by the National Sliding Scale. On 3rd March they agreed to a reduction of 2s. 6d. (12½p) in total but did not return to work until

Tuesday 4th April as, in the words of the *North Wales Weekly News* of 6th April: 'Differences afterwards arose concerning the appointment of an inspector as traffic superintendent, an appointment that was resented by the men'. Whilst the dispute continued the company took the opportunity to lift the rails on the abandoned West Shore section and use them to relay the track between Hooson's Corner and St John's Church.

General improvements were also continued throughout this period and the track-doubling programme was completed; the twin tracks now stretched from Greenfield Road, Colwyn Bay to Mostyn Street, Llandudno. The last section of the line to be so treated was the stretch in Colwyn Bay from the railway bridge to the Council offices in Conway Road; the opportunity to carry out the work came in 1929 after the UDC had widened the road. (It should be noted in passing that as from 1st April, 1926 Colwyn Bay & Colwyn Urban District was retitled the Urban District of Colwyn Bay; on 20th September, 1934 Colwyn Bay was incorporated as a Borough and during the Charter Week celebrations one of the trams was especially decorated and, in the words of the *North Wales Pioneer* of 25th September, 'evoked well-merited praise'.)

Looking back from our modern-day vantage point it is not difficult to see that this period held the key to the future of the tramway. Events which took shape then were directly responsible for the eventual demise of the line a quarter of a century later, for in those inter-war years came the assertion of the motor bus for a place in the scheme of things. (To anyone acquainted with the broad outlines of tramway history this turn of events will be a familiar one.) Motor buses had been licensed by Llandudno UDC since the early years of the 20th century and were operated by a firm known as the Llandudno Motor and Garage Co. Ltd (registered on 13th February, 1907); by World War I the Llandudno Coaching Co. Ltd and Messrs Jarvis & Woodyatt had joined the fray as the clamour for more licences rose.

Competition to the LCBER between Llandudno and Colwyn Bay – and even within those two towns – was inevitable. In 1926 Colwyn Bay UDC (nursing memories of never having got the better of the tramway company by building the Colwyn Bay section of the line itself?) obtained powers in a general Act of Parliament to operate buses along the sea front; not to be caught on the hop the company began to consider running its own bus services there but in 1929 was forced to announce a tactical withdrawal. In the face of both private competition and the increasing difficulties of operating through growing holiday traffic along a narrow section of the main North Wales coast road (the A55) the decision was taken to curtail tram services at the end of the double-track section at the Greenfield Road–Conway Road junction. As from 22nd September, 1930 the single-track section to Old Colwyn was abandoned and Crosville Motor Services Ltd stepped smartly in to fill the gap; the tramway company did however have the foresight to obtain a licence to run buses on the rest of the route if ever the tramway was forced by unforeseen circumstance to close. The line now consisted, in its final form, of 5.72 miles of double track and 0.82 miles of single track, totalling 6.54 miles in all. (After the closure of the Old Colwyn section, all services terminated outside St Paul's Church for some weeks

Toastrack 19 climbing the Little Orme in the summer of 1938 with a full complement of passengers in the care of the immaculately-clad crew. *D.W.K. Jones*

No. 11 (ex-Bournemouth) working 'wrong line' at Penrhyn Bay after the track damage suffered during the 1948–9 winter. *D.W.K. Jones*

until the north side of the roadway at the new terminus had been widened sufficiently to enable traffic to pass either side of a tramcar standing on the short terminal stub in the middle of the road.)

At the start of the 1930s the company's Directors were Balfour, Lovering, Williams and a new Chairman, Col Sir Joseph Nall, DSO; by this date Lovering was also a Delhi tramway and Barbados electricity Director whilst Nall was on the Boards of several bus and tramway companies – the latter including those of Leamington & Warwick, Cheltenham, Mansfield and Nottinghamshire & Derbyshire (the last three as Chairman) – as well as running his own large family road haulage business of Joseph Nall & Co. Ltd based in Manchester. By the end of 1937 both Williams and Balfour had left to be replaced by R.E. Birch.

Crosville was at this time busy strengthening its hold upon the bus services of the area: on 1st May, 1930 it took over Brookes Bros of Rhyl, on 1st August North Wales Silver Motors Ltd of Llandudno and, on 18th February of the following year, the Llandudno Coaching & Carriage Co. Ltd. It must now have started to become clear that the trams would, sooner or later, be displaced by buses. The fact that it was later rather than sooner was simply due to the cost involved in resurfacing the roadway after the removal of the tracks; this same obstacle effectively blocked the company's 1931 proposal to replace the trams with trolleybuses, as was then current Balfour, Beatty policy (so retaining use of the overhead equipment). It was decided instead to continue with the trams, replacing most of the existing ailing stock with more modern second-hand cars from other systems. Accordingly in 1932 and 1933 five single-deck cars were purchased from Accrington Corporation and in 1936 ten double-deck cars were bought from Bournemouth. (BoT permission to use double-deck vehicles between Old Colwyn and Penrhyn Bay had been obtained in 1916; this was now extended to the whole system providing no passengers were carried on upper decks over the exposed stretch of line at Penrhyn Bay and Penrhynside if the wind speed exceeded 50 mph.)

General view of the depot at Rhos on Sea at 3.40 pm on Wednesday 29th May, 1946.
Left to right: Nos. 17, 13, 23, 11, 1, 10.   *E.C. Haywood*

UNTIL FURTHER NOTICE.

LLANDUDNO & COLWYN BAY ELECTRIC RAILWAY LIMITED
TIME TABLE

COLWYN BAY AND LLANDUDNO—WEEK DAYS

Colwyn Bay						7 20	7 30	7 40	7 50	8	0 8	10 8	20 8	30 8	40 8	50 9	0		9 20	9 30	9 40	9 50	10	0 10	10 10	20 10	30 10 40 10 50
Rhos-on-Sea						7 28	7 38	7 48	7 58	8	8 8	18 8	28 8	38 8	48 8	58 9	8		9 28	9 38	9 48	9 58	10	8 10	18 10	28 10	38 10 48 10 58
Church Road	6 50	7	0 7	10 7	20 7	32 7	42 7	52 8	2 8	12 8	22 8	32 8	42 8	52 9	2 9	12	9 32	9 42	9 52	10	2 10	12 10	22 10	32 10	42 10 52 11 2
Penrhyn Side	6 56	7	6 7	16 7	26 7	38 7	48 7	58 8	8 8	18 8	28 8	38 8	48 8	58 9	8 9	18	9 38	9 48	9 58	10	8 10	18 10	28		
Queen's Road	7	3 7	13 7	23 7	33 7	45 7	55 8	5 8	15 8	25 8	35 8	45 8	55 9	5 9	15 9	25	9 45	9 55	10	5 10	15 10	25 10	35		
Hooson's Cnr.	7	9 7	19 7	29 7	39 7	51 8	1 8	11 8	21 8	31 8	41 8	51 9	1 9	11 9	21 9	31	9 51	10	1 10	11 10	21 10	31 10	41		
Llandudno W. Shore	7 15	7 25	7 35	7 45	7 55	8	5 8	15 8	25 8	35 8	45 8	55 9	5 9	15 9	25 9	35	9 55	10	5 10	15 10	25 10	35 10	45		

LLANDUDNO AND COLWYN BAY—WEEK DAYS

Llandudno W. Shore					7 15	7 25	7 35	7 45	7 55	8	5 8	15 8	25 8	35 8	45 8	55 9	5	9 15	9 25	9 35	9 45	9 55	10	5 10 15 10 25 10 35 10 50
Hooson's Cnr.					7 19	7 29	7 39	7 49	7 59	8	9 8	19 8	29 8	39 8	49 8	59 9	9	9 19	9 29	9 39	9 49	9 59	10	9 10 19 10 29 10 39 10 54
Queen's Road					7 25	7 35	7 45	7 55	8	5 8	15 8	25 8	35 8	45 8	55 9	5	9 15	9 25	9 35	9 45	9 55	10	5 10	15 10 25 10 35 10 45 11 0
Penrhyn Side					7 32	7 42	7 52	8	2 8	12 8	22 8	32 8	42 8	52 9	2	9	9 25	9 35	9 45	9 55	10	5 10 15 10 25 10 35 10 45 11 0
Church Road	7	5 7	15 7	25 7	37 7	47 7	57 8	7 8	17 8	27 8	37 8	47 8	57 9	7 9	17 9	27	9 37	9 47	9 57	10	7 10 17 10 27 10 37 10 47 10 57 11 12
Rhos-on-Sea	7	9 7	19 7	29 7	42 7	52 8	2 8	12 8	22 8	32 8	42 8	52 9	2 9	12 9	22 9	32	9 42	9 52	10	2 10 12 10 22 10 32 10 42		
Colwyn Bay	7	20 7	30 7	40 7	50 8	0 8	10 8	20 8	30 8	40 8	50 9	0 9	10 9	20 9	30 9	40	9 50	10	0 10 10 10 20 10 30 10 40 10 50			

Augmented at Week-ends and Holiday Periods.
* Subject to slight alteration to meet the requirements of Llandudno Theatres.
† These cars connect with the Club Train at Colwyn Bay.

COLWYN BAY AND LLANDUDNO—SUNDAYS

Colwyn Bay		12 15		12 46		1 16	1 32	1 48	2	4		8 12	8 28	8 44	9	0 9 16	9 32	9 48	10	4 10 20 10 36 10 50
Rhos-on-Sea		12 25		12 54		1 26	1 42	1 58	2 14			8 22	8 38	8 54	9 10	9 26	9 42	9 58	10 14	10 20 10 40 11 0
Penrhyn Side	11 53	12 35	12 48	1	4	1 20	1 36	1 52	2	8 2 24		8 32	8 48	9	4 9 20	9 36	9 52	10	8	
Queen's Road	12	0 12 41	12 55	1	11	1 26	1 42	1 58	2 14	2 30		8 38	8 54	9 10	9 26	9 42	9 58	10 14		
Hooson's Cnr.	12	5 12 47	1	1	1 17	1 32	1 48	2	4 2 20	2 36		8 44	9	0 9 16	9 32	9 48	10	4 10 20		
Llandudno W. Shore	12	9 12 51	1	5	1 21	1 36	1 52	2	8 2 24	2 40		8 48	9	4 9 20	9 36	9 52	10	8 10 24		

LLANDUDNO AND COLWYN BAY—SUNDAYS

Llandudno W. Shore		12 10		12 52	1	6	1 22	1 38	1 54	2 10		8 18	8 34	8 50	9	6 9 22	9 38	9 54	10 10 10 26
Hooson's Cnr.		12 14		12 56	1	12	1 28	1 44	2	0 2 16		8 24	8 40	8 56	9 12	9 28	9 44	10	0 10 16 10 32
Queen's Road		12 20		1	2	1 18	1 34	1 50	2	6 2 22		8 30	8 46	9	2 9 18	9 34	9 50	10	6 10 22 10 38
Penrhyn Side		12 28		1 10	1 26	1 42	1 58	2 14	2 30			8 38	8 54	9 10	9 26	9 42	9 58	10 14	10 30 10 46
Rhos-on-Sea	12	5 12 36	1	5	1 20	1 36	1 52	2	8 2 24	2 40		8 48	9	4 9 20	9 36	9 52	10	8 10 24 10 40 10 56
Colwyn Bay	12 15	12 45	1	15	1 30	1 46	2	2 2 18	2 34	2 50		8 58	9 14	9 30	9 46	10	2 10 18 10 34 10 50	

The Company will endeavour to conform to the above Time Table, but will not hold themselves responsible for any delay or inconvenience caused by unforseen circumstances.

April, 1933.

W. G. HAMILTON, A.M.I.E.E., General Manager.

Printed by Leigh & Williams, Ltd. Colwyn Bay.

LCBER summer timetable for 1933.

On the face of it the tramway was enjoying a period of reasonable prosperity: it had a new Manager (W.G. Hamilton, AMIEE of Bournemouth from 1931), a second source of power (Colwyn Bay's new power station opened in 1932 and current for the Colwyn Bay section of the line was now taken from here), new wiring (in 1938 the entire overhead was renewed) and a fleet of 'new' cars. The real truth was slightly different: an important section of the line had had to be abandoned, only 10 or more-year-old cars could be afforded and, when all was said and done, it was only the cost of its abandonment that was keeping the line open. The special circumstances of the war years about to come only warded off the inevitable for a little longer.

The following table gives some basic details of the tramway's operations during World War I and the inter-war period.

Year ending 31st December	Traffic receipts	Working expenditure	Passengers carried	Car miles
1914*	£15,672	£ 8,404	1,663,887	273,467
1915*	£17,482	£ 9,219	2,061,106	288,152
1916*	£18,773	£10,167	2,128,680	301,603
1917*	£18,061	£10,011	2,050,089	267,449
1918*	£23,249	£12,160	2,329,358	252,080
1919*	£30,633	£24,270	2,879,636	282,070
1920*	£34,024	£26,308	2,903,646	292,380
1921*	£38,035	£27,417	2,327,337	264,164
1922*	£34,577	£25,164	2,231,983	306,871
1923*	£35,351	£27,354	2,444,170	361,588
1924*	£29,916	£26,822	2,193,579	372,935
1925*	£28,029	£23,450	2,353,966	410,803
1926**	£26,704	£26,697	2,446,228	462,516
1927	£22,505	£21,662	2,049,657	428,353
1928	£20,663	£20,980	2,250,829	442,910
1929	£20,910	£20,773	2,436,826	464,472
1930	£15,830	£18,161	1,993,640	387,392
1931	£14,635	£14,840	1,779,505	406,533
1932	£17,415	£15,899	2,119,262	487,843
1933	£19,700	£16,718	2,399,831	437,698
1934	£19,948	£16,353	2,519,192	424,478
1935	£19,341	£17,446	2,485,782	428,207
1936	£18,943	£16,702	2,541,569	423,459
1937	£20,086	£16,152	2,625,259	417,992
1938	£19,392	£16,202	2,574,205	420,500
1939	£20,056	£16,286	2,657,586	405,793

*   year ending 30th November.
**   13 months ending 31st December.

The 1920s depot staff line up for the photographer against a pair of the original cars . . .
Courtesy LCBER Society

. . . and against the shed wall.
Courtesy LCBER Society

No. 7 (ex-Bournemouth) on 21st November, 1955 about to leave the interlaced section of track in Conway Road, Colwyn Bay. *D.W.K. Jones*

Service car No. 13 passing the 1951 Light Railway Transport League special in Rhos. *D.W.K. Jones*

Chapter Six
World War Two and after

Throughout the duration of World War II the tramway continued its uninterrupted run of daily operation, the only direct effect of the hostilities being the blacking-out of the tram windows and the use of blue bulbs for internal lighting in accordance with the blackout regulations. Indirectly though the war had many effects upon the tramway – the principal one being a welcome increase in passenger figures caused by the influx into the area of several Government offices and many service personnel. A further bounty was traffic deserting to the tramway from the reduced bus services – one of the casualties of petrol and fuel oil rationing. Another result of the rationing was the introduction of various special services, one of which was a 'staff car' for employees returning home after evening duties; another was an extra shuttle service (the 'Llandudno Local') between the West Shore and Craig-y-Don while still another was the hiring-out of cars on Sundays for private excursions. The last major change caused by the war was one repeated on countless other tramway systems in Britain: the employment of conductresses.

Although never on the receiving end of any war damage, three incidents did occur on the tramway during this period which need mentioning. The first took place in the spring of 1943 when gales and heavy seas caused the collapse of the old sea wall beside the reserved track along Penrhyn Bay between the Little Orme and Rhos; several tons of debris were deposited on the line. Similar, though less damaging, events had occurred in 1927 and 1933 and in October 1945 exactly the same thing happened again, only this time with more serious results: the track formation was so encroached upon that the seaward track of the two was declared unsafe and for two weeks, whilst the damage was repaired, single-line working was in force over the inner track between the crossovers at Penrhynside and the depot. The third and final incident took place in November of the same year when car No. 16 (originally No. 6 of 1907) ran a hot axlebox, caught fire and had to be scrapped.

The tramway emerged from the war years in optimistic mood, promptly ordering in 1946 two second-hand double-deck cars from Darwen Corporation. These were of a far more modern design than anything possessed by the LCBER (they dated from just before the war) and were allocated new numbers of 23 and 24; they were to be the last items of rolling stock to come to the line. After regauging from 4 ft, trials, driver training and so forth, a Ministry of Transport test was held on the cars on 14th April, 1948 with an outcome that came as both a shock and a disappointment to the company. On account of their high-sided closed bodywork the new cars would not be permitted to operate in public service on the section through Bodafon Fields, over Penrhyn Hill, along the coastal stretch and on to the depot at Rhos because of the possible danger of their turning over in windy conditions. Consequently No. 23 entered service on Thursday 22nd April on the Llandudno Local between Nant-y-Gamar Road and the West Shore, followed by No. 24 on a similar shuttle service between the depot and the Colwyn Bay terminus.

Meanwhile the never-ending task of maintaining the permanent way to the required standard continued; the first major section to be tackled after the war was that through Rhos from the depot to Colwyn Crescent. One track at a time was relaid, resulting in single-line working throughout 1946 and 1947; one track was relaid on a new concrete bed and the other on ballasted sleepers – possibly to facilitate future singling – both then being metalled over.

The stretch along Penrhyn Bay was by now a notorious trouble-spot for during the winter of 1948–9 the line was once again damaged by heavy seas and the ground under the seaward track was washed away. It was again necessary to put single-line working into operation while the formation was repaired, this time aided by new crossovers laid at Maesgwyn Road and the Golf House (at either end of the affected section) so as to reduce disruption of normal services to a minimum. Four winters later, in 1952–3, the story was repeated yet again. After a start had been made on making a more solid defence against the sea by hauling boulders up the beach with a winch fitted to car No. 17, the attempt was abandoned as too difficult and too costly. From then on only the nearside track was used between the two loops and a single overhead wire was installed using poles and bracket arms acquired from Stockport Corporation in 1951 as spares. The outer track was left to disappear under piles of shingle and suffer piecemeal obliteration in the construction of a new sea wall.

The ex-Stockport poles were not the only second-hand items to be purchased for the tramway to replace aged and failing equipment. In November 1952 more tubular poles, a number of wheel tyres and several items of depot equipment were bought from Birmingham Corporation; the following year a number of Dick, Kerr type 30B motors, gears, axles and wheels, and a quantity of seat cushions were obtained from the same source. In 1954 four sets of Dick, Kerr K4 controllers came from Sunderland Corporation. (See Chapter 10 for details of the subsequent modifications to the LCBER cars.) These spares were made available by the closure of the Birmingham system in 1953 and Sunderland in 1954 – both ominous omens for the LCBER.

Several minor track alterations also took place during the early 1950s. In November 1952 the single-track section in Mostyn Street was lifted and relaid; whilst this work was in progress cars for Colwyn Bay commenced their journey from Mostyn Broadway with the West Shore being served by a shuttle from Gloddaeth Street. August 1953 saw the re-sleepering of the reserved section between Nant-y-Gamar Road and Penrhyn Hill, the transfer of the trailing crossover from the Colwyn Crescent end of Penrhyn Avenue to Mostyn Broadway and the laying of a sewer under the Rhos end of the toll road. (While this latter work was being carried out passengers and crew walked over the break to change cars.) The crossover move was done in order to deal with a much-needed increase in traffic: cars could now terminate in Mostyn Broadway by the Grand and Arcadia Theatres and pick

Double-deckers Nos. 12 and 7 (both ex-Bournemouth) and works car No. 23 in the car shed in May 1951 with their trolley poles in the normal position facing towards the entrance.

D.W.K. Jones

up the queueing crowds bound for Colwyn Bay. Following complaints by the Council in 1953 over the state of the track and roadways in Llandudno the company gave an assurance that future repairs would be more substantial; in 1954 sections of Mostyn Broadway were relaid and retarred.

To return to the problems of the Penrhyn Bay sea wall: in the summer of 1953 the local authorities involved were given a government grant to construct a new set of sea defences (including the new sea wall mentioned above). This work was carried out during 1953, resulting in the permanent singling of the line at that point; after its completion a public enquiry was held at the beginning of 1954 to hear objections from the LCBER and local residents. The latter claimed that the cost of the work had been excessive and for the money spent a promenade could easily have been incorporated into the structure; the tramway company on the other hand claimed that it *was* the authorities' intention to construct a new coast road along the sea wall, thus depriving the company of the tolls it collected on the existing roadway. In reply the authorities denied any intent to construct a new road but carefully left their options open by admitting that the work done would facilitate any construction of a coast road at a later date. All of which added fuel to the company's growing belief that Llandudno UDC was anxious to see the back of the trams – hence its continual complaints about the state of the track and the roads.

The Council was not the only body that would profit by the closure of the tramway. The Chairman of the LCBER Co., Sir Joseph Nall, announced traffic figures for 1953 as follows:

Passengers	2,744,593
Receipts	£31,137
Loss	£1,222

One hopes that Sir Joseph – to give him his full title, Colonel Sir Joseph Nall, DSO, TD, DL, JP, M Inst T – gained some small measure of satisfaction from his being created a baronet in the coming New Year's Honours List for on 10th November, 1954, at the LCBER Ltd's annual general meeting in London, he announced even worse figures for that year:

Passengers	2,697,994
Receipts	£30,906
Loss	£3,004

In view of the current financial state of the company the Directors were actively considering replacing the trams with motor buses. As the Chairman's statement to shareholders put it:

> The Directors have for some time been considering the advisability of substituting motor buses in place of trams, and as a first step towards this, application is being made to the Licensing Authority for the granting of a road service licence. It is considered that the operation of motor buses, although not possessing the present-day novelty of trams, would be more attractive to the travelling public and of benefit to the company.

The company now had four Directors, Messrs Nall, Lovering and Birch having been joined by Stanley Dudman, M Inst T in 1946; four years later the registered office had moved to Suffolk House, Laurence Pountney Hill, Cannon Street, London EC4. Birch left the Board in 1952, as did Lovering the following year; their replacement appointees were J.R. Amphlett as a Director and D.R.P. Baker as Company Secretary.

Appeals and proposals by tramway enthusiasts that a preservation body should step in (an almost unheard-of idea recently pioneered on the Talyllyn Railway), or that Llandudno UDC should purchase the line and run it summer seasons only – in much the same way as the Great Orme line – were made in a valiant but (as it soon became plain) futile effort to save the last 3 ft 6 in. gauge electric tramway – and the last privately-owned tramway – in the country from closure.

The trams the holidaymakers remember: toastrack 22 on Rhos Promenade during the 1920s.   *Courtesy LCBER Society*

The one that got away; loading No. 6 on the occasion of its rescue for preservation. *Below*: details of the bogie. *G.R. Thompson Collection*

Chapter Seven
Closure

On 14th September, 1955 came the long-expected announcement: despite the Directors' recognition of the 'novelty of trams' (what would that novelty be worth to Llandudno today?) the tramway was definitely to close before the year was out and to add weight to the decision a second-hand bus was purchased from the East Kent Road Car Co. Ltd for the purpose of training drivers. Circumstances however dictated otherwise and it became apparent that the trams would, after all, see in the New Year. The first delay was made evident on 12th October when the Chairman of the North Western Area Traffic Commissioners declared that the LCBER Ltd would have to agree to a joint bus timetable with Crosville and then have it approved by the Commissioners before the tramway's bus service could begin.

The second delay came on 1st November when a meeting was held in Colwyn Bay to decide the future of the track and roads used by the tramway; representatives of the company, the local authorities and the Ministry of Transport were present. The outcome of the meeting was that no decision could as yet be reached as to who was responsible for making good the roadways, though the local authorities remained unmoved from their conviction that, under the original 1898 Light Railway Order, the onus rested fairly and squarely on the tramway company.

At the same time it became imperative from the company's point of view to cease operations before the summer of 1956. The reason for this was a simple financial one: the company's contract with the Merseyside & North Wales Electricity Board (MANWEB) – which in 1947 had acquired the municipal power stations of both Llandudno and Colwyn Bay – for the supply of current for the overhead was due to expire then. MANWEB presented the company with a choice of two alternatives after the contract expired: either pay a new charge of £100 per day for the supply or else take over the generating plant from them and install it behind the depot. (It should be noted that MANWEB employed a full-time staff of eight men to operate this plant at its power stations in Cwm Road, Llandudno and Ivy Street, Colwyn Bay.) Neither of these alternatives was within the existing financial means of the company and a closure date of Saturday 24th March, 1956 was promptly announced. It was a case of cutting further losses as quickly as possible, then settling the thorny question of the track removal. Eight cars were originally allocated for service during 1956 (three ex-Accrington and five ex-Bournemouth) while the rest of the fleet would be withdrawn as soon as any maintenance became necessary. Two of the first to go were ex-Bournemouth cars Nos. 9 and 10, scrapped in January.

And so the appointed day of closure arrived. Not suprisingly, the trams were packed to capacity all day with local residents, tramway enthusiasts and other visitors – including a party of former Bournemouth tram drivers who had a chance to try their hands again at the controls of their old charges. The official part of the proceedings began with an evening cocktail party at the Imperial Hotel, Llandudno, hosted by the company's Deputy Chairman,

Mr Stanley Dudman. Meanwhile the official 'last car', ex-Bournemouth No. 8, was brought up from the depot under the guidance of driver Dick Hughes and conductor Bob Morgan – long-standing employees for 39 and 37 years respectively. At 10.20 pm the official party, consisting of representatives of the Company, the local authorities, the police and Crosville Motor Services – totalling a hundred or so in all – clambered aboard No. 8 outside the North Western Hotel on Mostyn Broadway. With Chief Inspector J.E. Woolley at the controls and watched by a crowd of on-lookers, the loaded tram moved off towards the West Shore terminus, closely following No. 4 which carried the tramway's last fare-paying passengers.

Leaving the West Shore to the strains of 'Auld Lang Syne' from the crowd, No. 8 travelled back to the North Western Hotel and on through Llandudno towards the Little Orme. Here the Chairman of Llandudno UDC, Councillor John Owen, took over the controls for the stretch up to the depot. No. 8 paused here while the controls were handed over to the Mayor of Colwyn Bay, Councillor Edward Hughes, for the final run down to the Greenfield Road terminus, followed by a wide assortment of other road users. Car No. 3, minus seat cushions, was hurriedly substituted for No. 4 at the depot as that car's other controller had failed at the West Shore meaning that it had had to be driven from the rear end all the way to the depot! The arrival at, and subsequent departure from, Colwyn Bay were witnessed by another large crowd and a second convoy made its way along behind No. 8, this time returning to the depot which it reached about 1.00 am. Passengers for Llandudno were taken on from there by one of the company's buses although many preferred to walk back along the tracks to pay their last respects to the LCBER.

So died the tramway.

The last car, 24th March, 1956: No. 8 (ex-Bournemouth) outside the Grand Theatre in Llandudno in the company of No. 3 (ex-Accrington). *Lens of Sutton*

Chapter Eight
Epilogue

Thus it was on 25th March, 1956 that the LCBER Ltd became a bus operator with six double-deck buses painted dark red and cream – a livery which ironically came close to the tramway's original maroon and cream as they plied their trade between Llandudno and Colwyn Bay, faithfully adhering to the former tramway route and deviating only slightly at the sections of reserved track in Bodafon Fields and Glan-y-Mor road. Not so faithfully adhered to was the agreement with Crosville over such small things as timetables which, according to the local authorities, residents and press, were chiefly remarkable by their absence! Officially, the original service was every 10 minutes, later reduced to 15 minutes as a result of the Suez Crisis (and later still to 20 minutes).

By July – in time for the holiday season – the bus fleet had been enlarged to 13 service vehicles, made up of two Daimler double-deckers purchased second-hand from Newcastle-upon-Tyne Corporation and 11 Guy Arab double-deckers, also second-hand, from Southdown Motor Services Ltd in Sussex. (A detailed fleet list is given in Appendix 2.)

Messrs Walter & Co. of Oldham and Conway quickly went about their contracted task of dismantling, destroying and generally disposing of the carcase of the tramway. The Tramway Museum Society opened a fund to acquire car No. 6 (ex-Bournemouth No. 85) but if a very generous and big-hearted Mr A. Richardson of Rhyl had not stepped in, paid the asking price of £75 and presented the tram to the Museum of British Transport at Clapham, one wonders if No. 6 would have been saved from the fate of its shedmates. Stripped of anything of scrap value, anything saleable, the bodies were unceremoniously burnt outside the depot. All, that is, except Nos. 23 and 24, the two ex-Darwen cars: their steel bodies survived through the summer before receiving the scrapman's torch.

Although the overhead wires went within a month of the tramway's closure, the track lingered on – to the considerable annoyance of Llandudno and Colwyn Bay local authorities who wished to see its speedy removal. The reason for the delay was quite simple: the LCBER Ltd did not have the money to pay for the lifting of the track and the subsequent restoration of the roads. The company claimed that if it *did* decide to lift the track (presumably its scrap value would cover the cost of this part of the operation) it saw no reason to make good the roads since – undeniably – their condition in that broken state would still be better than it was in 1906! The two councils were not unnaturally inclined to a somewhat different view and began to make threatening noises regarding seeking of powers to lift the track, repair the roads and hand the tramway company the bill – whereupon the company decided not to go out fighting and handed over £5,000 to the councils to do the whole job; this sum was effectively increased by the scrap value of the track.

The subsequent roadworks occasioned minor alterations to the company's bus route and services; the buses, known familiarly as the 'Red buses', were

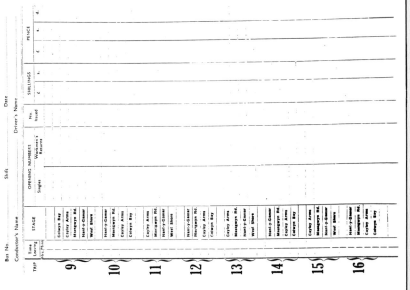

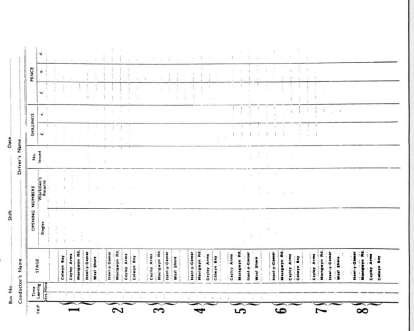

based at the former tram depot which had been adapted for the purpose. Greater problems arose from the competition with Crosville and the smaller concern soon found itself being squeezed out of existence. In April 1961 the company announced that it was giving up the struggle and the last LCBER buses ran on 27th May, by which date another three Guy Arabs had been added to the fleet as replacement vehicles; one from Southdown and two from East Kent. The next day the service was taken over by Crosville who had purchased the company's goodwill for £40,000.

There was now little reason for the continuing existence of the LCBER Ltd. All that was left was the Penrhyn Bay toll road and, in the face of the local authorities' desire to improve the public roads in the area to serve the growing residential development, the company decided to dispose of its remaining assets. Accordingly, on 14th November, 1961, the LCBER Ltd went into voluntary liquidation, paying to its shareholders 10s. (50p) per 10s. preferred share and ¼d. (0.1p) per 1s. (5p) deferred share. (It is believed that the toll road had ceased to generate any revenue since about April after the toll gate attendant fell ill and was not replaced.) The company's last three Directors at the close were Messrs Amphlett, Baker and Dodman; Dodman had been Chairman since Nall retired in 1958 and Baker had become a Director the year before that.

Today the urban development which took place during the tramway's life continues unabated; Llandudno's housing estates now extend alongside the route of the line to the West Parade and to Craig-y-Don. As so often with tramways, as opposed to railways, traces of their erstwhile existence disappear quickly after closure and the case of the LCBER is no exception. The street sections are now just streets with no hint that they were once more than that whilst the reserved sections have undergone a variety of changes. The Bodafon Fields right of way has now reverted to the pasture from which it was taken with only a fence and hedge along one side of the decaying trackbed to indicate where the trams ran; a metal gate marks the point where the line crossed Nant-y-Gamar Road to enter the fields.

The reserved section on the descent of Penrhyn Hill has suffered more; construction of a split-level dual carriageway in 1971 completely obliterated the former trackbed alongside the original road, as the conversion of the old toll road to a promenade and public road had already done. This is now a built-up area, as is Glan-y-Mor Road. The old car shed remains in commercial use and has been a road parcels depot for many years; other than that Colwyn Bay, like Llandudno, has effectively removed all traces of the line that once served it so well. The only other structure of any size still left is the West Shore tram shelter which has been renovated recently by David Williams Ltd of Llandudno on behalf of its present owner, Aberconwy Borough Council (the successor to Llandudno UDC) with the help of a grant from CADW, the Welsh equivalent of English Heritage.

There the story appeared to end with the tramway becoming a fading memory for all those who had known it. But it does not quite end there: on 19th September, 1974 the Llandudno Tramway Society was formed to keep that memory alive by collecting relics of the line for an intended local transport museum. Although the Society's plan to secure the return of No. 6 to Llandudno has been defeated (at least for some time if not for ever) by the successful application by Bournemouth for custody of it following the 1973 closure of the museum at Clapham, the remains of ex-Northampton double-decker No. 21 were acquired from a Northamptonshire farm in 1977 and moved to North Wales for restoration. In October of the same year a quantity of original rails from the West Shore terminus were lifted by Aberconwy BC and sold to the Society. (These had apparently escaped lifting after that section of the line was officially closed, instead being merely tarred-over.) Although the search is still on for a suitable site, who knows? Perhaps – one day – Llandudno will hear the sound of electric trams once again.

Perhaps.

Old scrapped tram body in the Llandudno depot photographed from the top of a double-deck tramcar in August 1939.   *Peter Johnson Collection*

Chapter Nine
Operations

SERVICES

The tramway's very first timetable, which came into effect from the line's opening, showed services commencing from both ends (West Parade and Rhos Depot) at 9.00 am and operating at 30-minute intervals. (Until the extension of the line into Colwyn Bay in 1908 passengers between there and Rhos were conveyed at 3d. (1p) a time in horse-brakes by Messrs J.F. Francis & Sons, carriage proprietors of Colwyn Bay, under an agreement with the tramway company.) Journey time over the first section of the line opened was approximately 30 minutes; with the extension to Colwyn Bay this increased to 40 minutes and again to 50 minutes when Old Colwyn was reached. After the closure of this last extension journey time went back to roughly 40 minutes – actual times of different scheduled workings varied by a few minutes. When fully operational the normal pattern was for a 10-minute interval service in the summer, reduced to a 20-minute one in the winter months. Interspersed with these through cars were the two 'locals': shuttle services between West Parade and Nant-y-Gamar Road in Llandudno and between Rhos Depot and the terminus in Colwyn Bay.

Normal services commenced between 6.00 am and 7.00 am and finished between 10.00 pm and 11.00 pm (as with actual schedules, these times were subject to endless minor variations over the years but serve to give the general picture). The first car of the day was a workmen's special: under the 1898 Order the company was required to run at least one car in each direction every day (except Sunday) before 7.00 am and again after 5.30 pm, for the benefit of workmen who were to travel at a reduced rate.

Occasionally special chartered trips were run, these being in the early years for children's outings and in later years for tramway enthusiasts.

WORKING

As would be expected, different patterns of working were in force at different times of the year. During the winter, with its reduced traffic and services, most of the work was done by the single-deck cars with the double-deckers (when purchased) filling out where need be. In post-1936 summer months all the double-deck cars would be in service, together with the toastracks, while the single-deckers stayed in reserve – though at the height of the season the whole fleet would be in action and the timetable abandoned!

Generally speaking though each car – crewed by driver and conductor – would adhere to the timetable as far as possible; this usually meant a fairly continuous service from one terminus to the other and almost immediately back again.

FARES

The original fare structure, as laid down by the 1898 Order, was based upon a maximum rate of 1d. (0.5p) per mile or fraction thereof, though the company was permitted to charge 2d. (1p) for any distance between ½ mile

LLANDUDNO & COLWYN BAY ELECTRIC RLY. LTD.

Workmen's Weekly Tickets and Scholar's 5 & 6-Day Weekly Tickets

The above are issued by conductors and can also be purchased at the Car Depot, Rhos-on-Sea, in accordance with the scale of charges set out below.

Where the ordinary single Fares are	Workmen's Weekly are	Scholar's Weekly are	
		6 Days	5 Days
	s. d.	s. d.	s. d.
1d.	6	6*	...
2d.	1 0	9*	...
3d.	1 6	1 3*	...
4d.	2 0	1 6*	1 3*
5d.	2 6	2 0*	1 8*
6d.	3 0	2 3*	1 10½*
7d.	3 6	2 9*	2 3*
8d.	4 0	3 0	2 6

Workmen's and Scholar's Weekly Tickets are available for one outward and return journey **each day**, except those marked thus * which are available for two journeys per day, both outward and return.
Workmen's Weekly Tickets are only available before 9 a.m. for the outward journey.

Tramway Depot,
Rhos-on-Sea.

W. G. HAMILTON, A.M.I.E.E.,

February, 1933.   General Manager.

1933 concessionary fares table and workmen's 6d. weekly return ticket (grey).

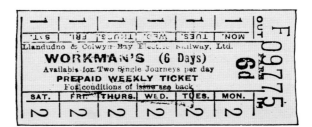

LLANDUDNO & COLWYN BAY ELECTRIC RAILWAY LIMITED

LLANDUDNO - PENRHYN BAY - RHOS-ON-SEA - COLWYN BAY

SINGLE FARES

1/1	11	10	9	7½	—	6½	5½	4	3	—	2	LLANDUDNO (West Shore)
11	10	9	7½	6½	—	5½	4	3	2	—	PALLADIUM or ST. JOHN'S CORNER CHURCH	
—	—	—	—	5½	—	4	—	2	—	NORTH WESTERN HOTEL		
—	—	—	—	—	4	—	—	—	QUEEN'S ROAD or CARMEN SYLVA ROAD			
10	9	7½	6½	5½	—	3	2	QUEEN'S ROAD or NANT-Y-GAMAR ROAD				
9	7½	5½	4	3	—	2	BRYN-Y-BIA ROAD (Llandudno Road End)					
7½	6½	5½	3	2	—	PENRHYNSIDE						
—	5½	4	—	—	LITTLE ORME CAFE							
6½	4	3	2	PENRHYN BAY (Maesgwyn Road)								
4	3	2	CHURCH ROAD									
3	2	RHOS-ON-SEA (Cayley Promenade or Colwyn Avenue)										
2	FIVEWAYS or KING'S ROAD											
COLWYN BAY (Bay View Road or Greenfield Road)												

WORKERS' DAILY RETURN FARES

1/5	1 4	1/3	1/2	1/0	11	10	7	—	LLANDUDNO (West Shore)
1/4	1/3	1/2	1/1	11	10	—	—	PALLADIUM CORNER or ST. JOHN'S CHURCH	
1/3	1/2	1/1	11	7	—	—	QUEEN'S ROAD or NANT-Y-GAMAR ROAD		
1/1	11	10	7	-	—	BRYN-Y-BIA ROAD (Llandudno Road End)			
1/0	10	7	—	—	PENRHYNSIDE				
11	—	—	—	MAESGWYN ROAD					
—	—	—	CHURCH ROAD						
—	—	COLWYN AVENUE or CAYLEY PROMENADE							
—	FIVEWAYS or KING'S ROAD								
COLWYN BAY (Bay View Road or Greenfield Road)									

Return Tickets at Workpeople's Fares rates are available to any bona-fide person travelling to work and scheduled to complete their journey at or before 9.0 a.m. The return journey may be taken at any time of the day. Workpeople's Tickets are not available on Sundays.

CHILDREN'S FARES

Children under FIVE years of age FREE, if not occupying a seat, accompanied by an Adult Fare Paying Passenger, providing that not more than one such child accompanies any passenger. Additional children, irrespective of age, MUST BE PAID FOR.

Children from 5 up to their 14th birthday half fare (unless otherwise stated), and also bona-fide children up to their 16th birthday during term time only, and then only to and from school, Sundays excepted, can travel at HALF ORDINARY ADULT FARES. Minimum Children's Fare 1½d. Half-pennies treated as pennies except in the case of the following adults fares, when the children's fare will be:—

Adult	Children
2½d.	1½d.
3d.	1½d.
4½d.	2½d.
6½d.	3½d.
8½d.	4½d.

SCHOLARS' 5-DAY WEEKLY TICKETS

Scholars' 5-Day Weekly Tickets are issued by Conductors between any two stages on Mondays and Tuesdays up to 2.0 p.m., where indicated on Fare Tables.

Scholars' Weekly Tickets are available during week of issue only for two outward and two inward journeys each day.

These tickets are available to bona-fide school children up to their 16th birthday (during term time only), and then only to and from school.

Where the ordinary Adult Single Fares are:	Scholars' 5-Day Weekly Tickets are:
2	1/8
2½	1/10
3	2/1
3½	2/3
4	2/5
5	2/11
5½	3/0
6	3/4
6½	3/6
7½	4/1
9	4/10
10	5/1

W. BUTTERWORTH,
General Manager.

Undated concessionary fares table (probably early 1950s).

SCHEDULE.

MAXIMUM RATES AND CHARGES FOR GOODS MATERIALS ARTICLES AND THINGS CONVEYED BY THE COMPANY ON THE RAILWAYS.

Animals.

For every horse mule or other beast of draught or burden fourpence per head per mile ;

For every ox cow bull or head of cattle threepence per head per mile ;

For calves pigs sheep and small animals one penny halfpenny per head per mile.

Goods.

For all coals coke culm charcoal cannel limestone chalk lime salt sand fireclay cinders dung compost and all sorts of manure and all undressed materials for the repair of public roads or highways twopence per ton per mile ;

For all iron ironstone iron ore pig iron bar iron rod iron sheet iron hoop iron plates of iron slabs billets and rolled iron bricks slag and stone stones for building pitching and paving tiles slates and clay (except fireclay) and for wrought iron not otherwise specially classed herein and for heavy iron castings including railway chairs twopence halfpenny per ton per mile ;

For all sugar grain corn flour hides dye woods earthenware timber staves deals and metals (except iron) nails anvils vices and chains and for light iron castings threepence per ton per mile ;

For cotton wools drugs manufactured goods and all other wares merchandise fish articles matters or things not otherwise specially classed herein fourpence per ton per mile :

For every carriage of whatever description one shilling per mile.

Small Parcels.

For any parcel not exceeding seven pounds in weight threepence ;

For any parcel exceeding seven pounds and not exceeding fourteen pounds in weight fivepence ;

For any parcel exceeding fourteen pounds and not exceeding twenty-eight pounds in weight sevenpence ;

For any parcel exceeding twenty-eight pounds and not exceeding fifty-six pounds in weight ninepence ;

For any parcel exceeding fifty-six pounds but not exceeding five hundred pounds in weight such sum as the Company may think fit ;

Provided that articles sent in large aggregate quantities although made up in separate parcels such as bags of sugar coffee meal and the like shall not be deemed small parcels but that term shall apply only to single parcels in separate packages.

Single Articles of Great Weight.

The Company shall not be bound to carry single articles of great weight but if they do carry such articles they may charge :—

For the carriage of any iron boiler cylinder or single piece of machinery or single piece of timber or stone or other single article the weight of which including the carriage shall exceed four tons but shall not exceed eight tons such sum as the Company may think fit not exceeding two shillings per ton per mile ;

For the carriage of any single piece of timber stone machinery or other single article the weight of which with the carriage shall exceed eight tons such sum as the Company may think fit.

Schedule of charges for non-passenger traffic on the LCBER as appended to the 1898 Light Railway Order.

Regulations as to Rates.

For animals goods or things conveyed on the railways for any less distance than two miles the Company may demand rates and charges as for two miles :

In computing the said rates and charges a fraction of a mile shall be deemed a mile :

For the fraction of a ton the Company may demand rates according to the number of quarters of a ton in such fraction and if there be a fraction of a quarter of a ton such fraction shall be deemed a quarter of a ton ;

With respect to all articles except stone and timber the weight shall be determined according to the imperial avoirdupois weight ;

With respect to stone and timber fourteen cubic feet of stone forty cubic feet of oak mahogany teak beech or ash and fifty cubic feet of any other timber shall be deemed one ton weight and so in proportion for any smaller quantity ;

In the case of goods and single articles of great weight the Company may demand such charges as are reasonable for loading and unloading the same and if any difference shall arise as to the reasonableness of any such charge the matter in difference shall be settled by the Board of Trade.

This Order made by the Light Railway Commissioners and modified by the Board of Trade is hereby confirmed in pursuance of Section 10 of the Light Railways Act 1896.

Given under the Seal of the Board of Trade this 2nd day of June, One thousand eight hundred and ninety-nine.

CHAS. T. RITCHIE,

President.

SEAL
OF THE
BOARD OF
TRADE.

FRANCIS J. S. HOPWOOD,

Assistant Secretary.

From Bathing Hut to Tramcar! A very early view near Penrhyn Bay.
Author's Collection

and 2 miles. The exception to this was the workmen's rate of ½d. per mile (minimum 1d). Passengers were allowed 28 lb. of accompanying luggage free of charge; other set rates could be applied at the discretion of the company for other commodities, the tramway being authorised to carry minerals, parcels, animals and general goods in addition to passengers.

This fare structure gave a basic end-to-end fare of 5d. (2p) when the first section of the line opened; this increased to 8d. (3.5p) when the line was fully opened. During the late 1920s fare increases were authorised (up to 1½d. per mile ordinary, 1d. per mile workmen's and an extra 75 per cent on the goods charges) but overall the changes had little effect. Indeed, the through fare later dropped to 7d. (3p) and was raised to 9d. (4p) only in 1953. Apart from these changes – and some minor stage alterations – the fares were remarkably consistent throughout the life of the tramway. Children under 14 years of age travelled at half-price; children under 3 rode free. Special weekly tickets for schoolchildren and workmen were issued, as well as workmen's day returns and, until 1941, a special 'excursion' return of 1s. (5p) was available between Llandudno and Colwyn Bay. Tickets used were of the Bell Punch variety (punches by Alfred Williamson Ltd).

TOLLS

Mention should be made of the tolls charged by the LCBER Ltd on its toll road section of the tramway along Penrhyn Bay. These tolls, for the return journey on the day of ticket issue only, were as follows:

Perambulator, light handcart or pedal cycle	1d.
Motor cycle on two wheels carrying one person	3d.
Motor cycle combination, or carrying two persons	6d.
Motor vehicle of seating capacity not exceeding eight passengers	1s.
Cart or carriage drawn by one horse	1s.
Light lorry or van not exceeding 5 tons gross loaded	1s.
Cart or carriage drawn by two horses	1s. 6d.

Heavy lorries, coaches and public service vehicles were prohibited from using the toll road – though when the company's own buses were introduced they used the road and from then on other PSVs were admitted upon payment of a charge of 2s. 6d. (12.5p). As regards the procedure for using the road, the notice at the toll house detailing the above charges also gave the following instruction:

> Drivers of vehicles passing through this gate are respectfully requested to see that the Toll-gate Keeper punches, in their presence, a ticket representing the value of the toll paid.

ACCIDENTS

There is no reason to suppose that the LCBER was not without its fair share of minor accidents; it does appear though to have been unlucky in being involved in at least three fatal ones. The first occurred on Friday 3rd July, 1914 when ten-year-old Trevor Roberts of Penrhyn Bay was knocked down by a tram outside the Golf Club at Rhos-on-Sea. Trevor was employed

LLANDUDNO AND COLWYN BAY ELECTRIC RAILWAY LIMITED

SUMMER TIME TABLE

COLWYN BAY (Greenfield Road) TO LLANDUDNO (West Shore)

MONDAYS TO SATURDAYS

		am	am	am	am	am	am	am	am		pm	pm	pm	pm	pm	pm	pm
COLWYN BAY (St. Paul's Church)	dept.	...	7 12	7 27	7 42	7 57	8 12	...	8 32		10 2	10 12	10 22	10 32	10 42	10 52	11 2
* King's Road	,,		7 16	7 31	7 46	8 1	8 16	...	8 35		10 5	10 14	10 24	10 34	10 44	10 54	11 4
RHOS (Cayley Promenade)	,,	6 50	7 19	7 34	7 49	8 4	8 19	...	8 39		10 9	10 18	10 28	10 38	10 48	10 58	11 8
* Church Road	,,	6 52	7 21	7 36	7 51	8 6	8 21	8 30	8 41		10 11	10 20	10 30	10 40	10 50	11 0	11 10
PENRHYN BAY (Golf Club)	,,	6 54	7 23	7 38	7 53	8 8	8 23	8 33	8 43		10 13	...					
* Little Orme Cafe	,,	6 56	7 25	7 40	7 55	8 10	8 25	8 36	8 46		10 16	...					
LLANDUDNO (Queen's Road)	,,	7 4	7 34	7 49	8 4	8 19	8 34	8 45	8 55		10 25	...					
* West Shore	arr.	7 11	7 41	7 56	8 11	8 26	8 41	8 53	9 3		10 33	...					

Then every 10 mins. until

SUNDAYS

		am	am	am	am	am	am	am	am	am	am	am		pm	pm	pm	pm
COLWYN BAY (St. Paul's Church)	dept.	...	...	8 32	...	8 52	9 2	9 12	9 22	9 32	9 42	9 52		9 52	10 2	10 12	10 32
* King's Road	,,			8 35	...	8 55	9 5	9 15	9 25	9 35	9 45	9 55		9 54	10 4	10 14	10 34
RHOS (Cayley Promenade)	,,	8 9	8 29	8 39	8 49	8 59	9 9	9 19	9 29	9 39	9 49	9 59		9 58	10 8	10 18	10 38
* Church Road	,,	8 11	8 31	8 41	8 51	9 1	9 11	9 21	9 31	9 41	9 51	10 1		10 0	10 10	10 20	10 40
PENRHYN BAY (Golf Club)	,,	8 13	8 33	8 43	8 53	9 3	9 13	9 23	9 33	9 43	9 53	10 3		...			
* Little Orme Cafe	,,	8 16	8 36	8 46	8 56	9 6	9 16	9 26	9 36	9 46	9 56	10 6		...			
LLANDUDNO (Queen's Road)	,,	8 25	8 45	8 55	9 5	9 15	9 25	9 35	9 45	9 55	10 5	10 15		...			
* West Shore	arr.	8 33	8 53	9 3	9 13	9 23	9 33	9 43	9 53	10 3	10 13	10 23		...			

Then every 10 mins. until

LLANDUDNO (West Shore) TO COLWYN BAY (Greenfield Road)

MONDAYS TO SATURDAYS

		am	am	am	am	am	am	am	am	am	am	am		pm	pm	pm
LLANDUDNO (West Shore)	dept.	...	...	7 13	...	7 43	7 58	8 13	...	8 28	8 43	...	8 55	10 15	10 25	10 35
* Queen's Road	,,	...	...	7 20	...	7 50	8 5	8 20	...	8 35	8 50	...	9 3	10 23	10 32	10 42
* Little Orme Cafe	,,	...	...	7 27	...	7 57	8 13	8 27	...	8 43	8 57	...	9 12	10 32	10 39	10 49
PENRHYN BAY (Golf Club)	,,			7 29	...	7 59	8 16	8 29	...	8 46	8 59	...	9 15	10 35	10 41	10 51
* Church Road	,,	7 0	7 15	7 31	7 45	8 1	8 18	8 31	8 40	8 48	9 1	9 18	9 18	10 38	10 43	10 53
RHOS (Cayley Promenade)	,,	7 3	7 18	7 33	7 48	8 3	8 21	8 33	8 43	8 51	9 3	9 12	9 21	10 41	10 46	10 56
* King's Road	,,	7 6	7 21	7 36	7 51	8 6	8 25	8 36	8 46	8 54	9 6	9 15	9 24	10 44	10 49	...
COLWYN BAY (Penrhyn Road)	arr.	7 9	7 24	7 39	7 54	8 9	8 28	8 39	8 49	8 58	9 9	9 18	9 28	10 48	10 53	

Then every 10 mins. until

SUNDAYS

		am	am	am	am	am	am	am	am	am	am	am		pm	pm	pm	pm
LLANDUDNO (West Shore)	dept.	...	...	...	8 35	...	8 55	9 5	9 15	9 25	9 35	9 45		9 45	9 55	10 5	10 15
* Queen's Road	,,	...	...	...	8 43	...	9 3	9 13	9 23	9 33	9 43	9 53		9 53	10 3	10 13	10 23
* Little Orme Cafe	,,	...	...	...	8 52	...	9 12	9 22	9 32	9 42	9 52	10 2		10 4	10 12	10 22	10 32
PENRHYN BAY (Golf Club)	,,				8 55	...	9 15	9 25	9 35	9 45	9 55	10 5		10 6	10 15	10 24	10 34
* Church Road	,,	8 20	8 40	8 50	8 58	9 10	9 18	9 28	9 38	9 48	9 58	10 8		10 6	10 18	10 26	10 36
RHOS (Cayley Promenade)	,,	8 22	8 42	8 52	9 1	9 12	9 21	9 31	9 41	9 51	10 1	10 11		10 8	10 20	10 28	10 38
* King's Road	,,	8 26	8 46	8 56	9 4	9 16	9 26	9 36	9 46	9 54	10 4	10 14		10 24	...		
COLWYN BAY (Penrhyn Road)	arr.	8 30	8 50	9 0	9 8	9 20	9 28	9 38	9 48	9 58	10 8	10 18		10 28	...		

Then every 10 mins. until

* The Company shall not be responsible for any delay or inconvenience due to any variations of the above Time Table.
Departure times from these stopping places are shown for the convenience of passengers and are approximate only.

W. BUTTERWORTH,
General Manager.

POWLSONS, PRINTERS, COLWYN BAY

LCBER summer timetable: undated but probably early 1950s. (Butterworth was the tramway's last General Manager.)

LLANDUDNO AND COLWYN BAY ELECTRIC RAILWAY LIMITED

WINTER TIME TABLE

COLWYN BAY (Greenfield Road) TO LLANDUDNO (West Shore)

MONDAYS TO SATURDAYS

		am	am	am	am	am	am	am	am	am	am	am	am	am	am	am	am	am
Greenfield Road	dept.	...	7 10	7 25	7 40	7 55	8 10	8 30	8 40	8 50	9 0	...	9 20	...	9 40	...	10 0	...	10 10
St. Paul's Church	,,	...	7 12	7 27	7 42	7 57	8 12	8 32	8 42	8 52	9 2	...	9 22	...	9 42	...	10 2	...	10 12
Rhos Promenade	,,	...	7 18	7 32	7 47	8 2	8 17	8 37	8 49	8 58	9 8	...	9 28	...	9 48	...	10 8	...	10 18
Church Road	arr.	6 50								8 59									10 19
Nant-y-Gamar Road	dept.											6 25			9 45		10 5		10 25
Queen's Road	,,	7 4	7 33	7 42	8 3	8 18	8 33	8 55	9 4	...	9 22	9 26	9 42	9 46	10 2	10 6	10 22	10 26	...
Palladium Corner	arr.										9 28		9 48		10 8		10 28		...
West Shore	arr.	7 11	7 41	7 56	8 11	8 26	8 41	9 3	9 13	...		9 34	...	9 54	...	10 14	...	10 34	...

MONDAYS TO SATURDAYS

		am	am	am	am	am		pm	pm	pm	pm	pm	pm	pm	pm	pm	pm	pm
Greenfield Road	dept.	10 20	...	10 30	10 40	10 50		6 10	6 20	6 30	6 40	7 0	7 35	8 5	8 35	9 5	9 35	10 5
St. Paul's Church	,,	10 22	...	10 32	10 42	10 52		6 12	6 22	6 32	6 42	7 2	7 37	8 7	8 37	9 7	9 37	10 7
Rhos Promenade	,,	10 28	...	10 38	10 48	10 58		6 18	6 28	6 38	6 48	7 8	7 42	8 12	8 42	9 13	9 43	10 13
Church Road	arr.			10 39		10 59	Repeated each hour until	6 19	6 29	6 39	6 49	7 9	7 43	8 13	8 43	9 14	9 44	10 14
Nant-y-Gamar Road	dept.			10 45														
Queen's Road	,,	10 42	10 46	...	11 2	...			6 45			7 2	7 26	7 56	8 26	8 56	9 26	9 56
Palladium Corner	arr.	10 48	...		11 8	...			6 51			7 8	...					
West Shore	arr.			10 54	...				6 53				7 33	8 3	8 33	9 3	9 33	10 3

LLANDUDNO (West Shore) TO COLWYN BAY (Greenfield Road)

MONDAYS TO SATURDAYS

		am	am	am	am	am	am	am	am	am	am	am	am	am	am	am	am	am
West Shore	dept.	...	...	7 13	...	7 43	7 58		8 13	8 28	8 45	9 5	9 15	...	9 35	...	9 55	...
Palladium Corner	,,	...	...	...	...	...	...		...	...	...	...	9 17	9 29	9 37	...	9 49	9 57
Queen's Road	,,	...	...	7 20	...	7 50	8 5		8 20	8 36	8 53	9 18	9 23	9 35	9 45	...	9 55	10 3
Nant-y-Gamar Road	arr.	...	...	...	...	...	...		...	...	...		9 24	...	9 44	...	...	10 4
Church Road	dept.	6 55	7 10	...	7 45	...	...		8 25	...	...	...	...	...	...	9 58	...	...	10 20
Rhos Promenade	,,	7 0	7 15	7 32	7 47	8 2	8 21	8 31	8 41	8 51	9 9	9 31	...	9 51	...	10 1	10 11	...	10 21
Railway Station, C. Bay	arr.	7 8	7 23	7 38	7 53	8 8	8 27	8 37	8 47	8 57	9 17	9 38	...	9 58	...	10 8	10 18	...	10 28

MONDAYS TO SATURDAYS

		am	am	am	am	am		pm	pm	pm	pm	pm	pm	pm	pm	pm	pm	pm
West Shore	dept.	...	10 15	...	...		5 55		...	6 55	...	7 35	8 5	8 35	9 5	9 35	10 5	
Palladium Corner	,,	10 9	10 17	...	10 29	...		8 9	6 29	6 57	7 9	7 37	8 7	8 37	9 7	9 37	Waits for Cinema	
Queen's Road	,,	10 15	10 23	...	10 35	...	6 3		6 15	6 35	7 3	7 15	7 42	8 12	8 42	9 12	9 42	10 12
Nant-y-Gamar Road	arr.	...	10 24	...	...	...		7 30										
Church Road	dept.	...	...	10 40	...		6 20	6 20		...	...	...	...	...	...	...	10 25	...
Rhos Promenade	,,	10 31	...	10 41	10 51		6 21	6 31		7 21	...	7 56	8 26	8 56	9 26	9 58	...	
Railway Station, C. Bay	arr.	10 38	...	10 48	10 58		6 28	6 38	6 58	7 28	...	8 3	8 33	9 3	9 33	10 3	...	

COLWYN BAY to LLANDUDNO

SUNDAYS

		am	am	am	am		pm	pm		pm	pm	pm
Greenfield Road	dept.	...	9 45	10 15	10 45		1 50	2 20		9 20	9 50	10 20
St. Paul's Church	,,	...	9 47	10 17	10 47		1 52	2 22		9 22	9 52	10 22
Rhos Promenade	,,	9 24	9 52	10 22	10 52	And every 30 mins. until	1 57	2 27	And every 30 mins. until	9 27	9 57	10 27
Queen's Road	,,	9 36	10 6	10 36	11 6		2 11	2 41		9 41	Depot only	
West Shore	arr.	9 43	10 13	10 43	11 13		2 18	2 48		9 48		

LLANDUDNO to COLWYN BAY

SUNDAYS

		am	am	am	am		pm	pm	pm		pm	pm
West Shore	dept.	...	9 45	10 15	10 45		1 50	2 20	2 50		9 20	9 50
Queen's Road	,,	...	9 52	10 22	10 52	And every 30 minutes until	1 57	2 27	2 57	And every 30 minutes until	9 27	9 57
Rhos Promenade	,,	9 35	10 6	10 36	11 6		2 11	2 41	3 11		9 41	10 11
Railway Stn., C. Bay	arr.	9 42	10 13	10 43	11 13		2 18	2 48	3 18		9 48	10 18

TO OPERATE FROM 3rd SUNDAY IN SEPTEMBER UNTIL SATURDAY BEFORE WHIT-SUNDAY

The Company shall not be responsible for any delay or inconvenience due to any variations of the above Time Table. Departure times from these stopping places are shown for the convenience of passengers and are approximate only.

POWLSONS, PRINTERS, COLWYN BAY

W. BUTTERWORTH.
General Manager.

LCBER winter timetable: undated but probably early 1950s.

after school hours as a caddie at the club and on the evening in question he walked out from behind a waiting tram and was hit by an approaching one, apparently disregarding (or misinterpreting) the warning bell that rang in the clubhouse whenever a tram approached.

The second accident involved a Holyhead woman, Dorothy Wall, who slipped and fractured her skull while trying to avoid a tram in Craig-y-Don on the evening of Thursday 9th February, 1928. The third fatality was again that of a child: this time a three-year-old boy, struck by a tram in Penrhyn Avenue on Friday 15th May, 1936 as he ran after his ball. The tram was travelling at just 10 mph but for a three-year-old child that was enough.

Car No. 24 at Colwyn Bay in June 1952.   H.L. Runnett

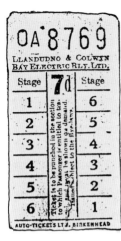

OA 8769

LLANDUDNO & COLWYN BAY ELECTRIC RLY. LTD.

Stage	**7d**	Stage
1		6
2		5
3		4
4		3
5		2
6		1

Ticket is to be punched in the section to which Passenger is entitled to travel, and must be shown on demand. Issued subject to the Bye-laws.

AUTO-TICKETS LTD. BIRKENHEAD

RITZ CAFÉ
AND RESTAURANT
39 MOSTYN STREET
LLANDUDNO
TELEPHONE 6711

GF 1957

LLANDUDNO & COLWYN BAY ELECTRIC RLY. LTD.

STAGE	**2d**	STAGE
1		8
2		7
3		6
4		5
5		4
6		3
7		2
8		1
DOG		DOG

Ticket is to be punched in the section to which Passenger is entitled to travel and must be shown on demand. Issued subject to the Bye-Laws.

AUTO-TICKETS LTD. BIRKENHEAD

PHOTOGRAPHS OF DISTINCTION

C. H. WILKINSON,
THE STUDIO,
Mostyn Avenue, Llandudno.
Phone: 6720.

Ez 6377

Llandudno and Colwyn Bay Electric Rly. Ltd.

FARE · 1D.

IN   BETWEEN   OUT

Queen's Hotel Old Colwyn and Penrhyn Road
Marine Road & St. Paul's Church (Station Road)
St Paul's Church and Whitehall Loop
King's Road Loop and Rhos Post Office
Rhos Post Office and Rhos Golf Club Entrance
Church Road and Penrhyn Circle
Penrhyn Circle and Penrhyn Hill
Penrhyn Hill and Nant-y-gamar Road
Nant-y-gamar Road and St. John's Chapel
Vaughan Street and Llandudno Terminus

DOG OR PARCEL

Must be shown for inspection or given up on demand. Issued subject to Bye-laws and Regulations.

Auto-Ticket & Co. Ltd. L'pool

Llandudno's Original & Popular Sweet Store,

45a Mostyn Street

The Harrogate Stores

LLANDUDNO

Depot for FARRAH'S Harrogate Toffee and Chocolates, etc.

OR 2939

LLANDUDNO & COLWYN BAY ELECTRIC RLY. LTD.

Stage	**1d**	Stage
1		12
2		11
3		10
4		9
5		8
6		7
7		6
8		5
9		4
10		3
11		2
12		1

Ticket is to be punched in the section to which Passenger is entitled to travel. Issued and must be shown on demand. Subject to the Bye-laws.

AUTO-TICKETS LTD. BIRKENHEAD

A selection of LCBER single tickets (with adverts on reverse). Colours used were: 1d. white, 1½d. brown (later brick red), 2d. buff, 3d. blue, 4d. yellow, 5d. green, 6d. mauve, 7d. pink, 8d. purple and 9d. light brick red.

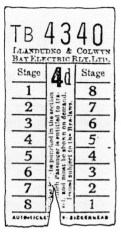

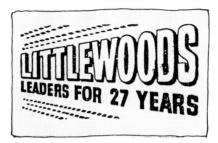

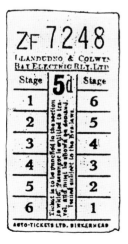

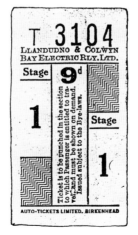

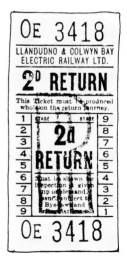

More LCBER tickets (again, all by Auto-Tickets Ltd of Birkenhead) including 2d. (grey) and 3d. (white) returns.

A crowded depot in November 1955 with three toastracks, original No. 17 (ex-14), a second-hand No. 2 (ex-Accrington), one of the ex-Darwen cars, No. 4 (ex-Bournemouth) and a tower wagon all managing to get into the picture.   *D.W.K. Jones*

A close-up view of the car shed with toastracks Nos. 19 and 21, 1907 car No. 18 (the renumbered 11) and No. 24 (ex-Darwen). Just visible on the right is one of the ex-Bournemouth cars.   *D.W.K. Jones*

Chapter Ten
Rolling Stock

As should be clear from the preceding chapters, the passenger cars used on the LCBER fell into three distinct groups. The first of these comprised the two ex-Canvey Island cars used for testing the line but never for public service; the second group was made up of the 22 cars ordered new for the line at various dates between 1907 and 1920 while the third consisted of the 17 second-hand vehicles purchased between 1932 and 1946 from a variety of sources. All three groups are dealt with in detail below in that order, followed by notes on their livery and indicators. The final section deals with the tramway's work cars.

EX-CANVEY ISLAND CARS

The first cars to run on the LCBER were the pair obtained in 1907 from the defunct Canvey Island Electric Tramways. These had been constructed in 1904 by the Brush Electrical Engineering Co. Ltd of Loughborough and were of a standard closed single-deck design. The 17 ft-long body (25 ft 6 in. over fenders) was mounted on a type 'A' truck with 30 in. diameter wheels on a 6 ft wheelbase. Seating was for up to 26 on longitudinal seats down the sides of the saloon.

When the Canvey Island venture ground to a halt in the same year that it got underway – 1904 – its stock of four cars was returned to Brush whence two were borrowed in January 1907 by Bruce Peebles for testing the Llandudno line so far constructed. Later the same year they were returned to their maker, never having been numbered or used in revenue service at Llandudno either. After standing in Brush's works yard for several years they were eventually broken up during World War I for their reusable components.

ORIGINAL CARS NOS. 1–14

The LCBER's first 14 cars were ordered and supplied in one batch for the opening of the line in 1907. Their bodies were constructed by the Midland Railway Carriage & Wagon Co. Ltd of Shrewsbury and the running gear manufactured and fitted by Mountain & Gibson Ltd of Bury. The bodies were single-deck saloons with monitor roofs and vestibuled end platforms with entrances each side. Internally the saloon was divided into two compartments, both with longitudinal rattan seating and polished oak and mahogany decor; total accommodation was given as 42 persons. The original allocation was given as one compartment for smokers and one for non-smokers but this arrangement was later dropped. (Judging by complaints made by members of the public at the time, the communicating door between the compartments was often left open or the division simply ignored anyway.)

Running gear consisted of a pair of four-wheel bogie trucks of the equal-wheel, swing bolster type, with two Bruce Peebles split-case 30 hp motors mounted outside the axles of each truck. The lifeguards were Mountain &

One of the original 1907 cars poses for a publicity photo before the opening of the line.

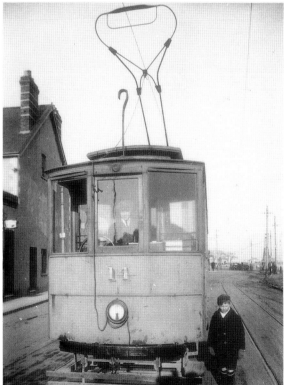

These photographs are the only two known to exist of the 1920s trials of No. 14 with a bow collector fitted at one end (presumably intended to eliminate dewirements).

Courtesy LCBER Society

Original car No. 4 of 1907 posed for its photograph at the bottom of Penrhyn Hill (looking towards the west).   *Oakwood Collection*

No. 14 well loaded, on a wet day, in Mostyn Street.   *Lens of Sutton*

Gibson's 'Simplex' type; the sanding gear was by Cummings and the magnetic brakes by Westinghouse. Hand-operated wheel brakes were also fitted, with a hand-wheel in each vestibule; a second, concentrically-mounted hand-wheel at each end provided a back-up system for applying the magnetic brakes – this was installed in view of the gradients over the Little Orme. Current collection was originally by way of a single trolley pole, but this was quickly found to be unsatisfactory and was subsequently replaced by two trolleys mounted near the centre of the roof and facing outwards. No further alterations were made to the cars until 1924–5 when the original motors were replaced by more powerful (40 hp) GE249 models and new B49CC controllers and magnetic brakes fitted, all from BTH, to replace the existing ones. In 1931 work started on filling-in one of the side entrances on each end platform.

At the close of the 1932 summer season Nos. 1–5 were withdrawn and scrapped after all reusable parts had been removed, including six bogies for use with the ex-Accrington trams (see below). In 1936 Nos. 6, 10, 11 and 14 were renumbered to follow consecutively from the 'new' ex-Accrington and Bournemouth cars (see below) and became Nos. 16, 19, 18 and 17 respectively; the remaining cars of the batch (i.e. original Nos. 7, 8, 9, 12 and 13) were then all withdrawn, stripped and scrapped. The lower saloon of one of these was cut in half to make two shelters for the stops at Bryn-y-Bia Road and the bottom of Penrhyn Hill on the Colwyn side. Of the quartet of survivors No. 19 was earmarked for conversion to a toastrack vehicle and was reduced to its steel frame and floor, but was finally stripped and scrapped in 1937 (one report says 1941) after the conversion was deemed impracticable; No. 16 was scrapped after being damaged by fire in November 1945 (see Chapter 6) while Nos. 17 and 18 survived until the closure in 1956 (though by this time No. 17 was out of use). Final modifications to these cars included the installation of lifeguards between the trucks and the permanent closing of the eight drop windows on each side.

(When it is stated here that a tram was scrapped it should be understood that it was the normal practice to strip it first of all parts which had any resale value, or could be used as spares – hence the survival of a wide variety of relics, especially those gathered by the Llandudno Tramway Society or, remarkably, still carrying out their original functions on another line as detailed in Appendix 3.)

ORIGINAL CARS NOS. 15–18

Known variously as 'Yankee' or 'winter cars' (their reduced capacity and enclosed bodywork made them suitable for that season's workings), the second batch of cars ordered for the tramway was built in 1909 and delivered in September of that year by the United Electric Car Co. Ltd of Preston. Running gear was again by Mountain & Gibson. The bodywork was unique for this country: a main saloon with eight drop windows each side, fully-vestibuled end platforms and a monitor roof; each platform had a seat for two passengers on the closed side opposite the entrance. Sliding doors gave access to the saloon from the end platforms; one end of the saloon was

Original 1907 car No. 18 (formerly 11) in 1949 with second-hand No. 3 (ex-Accrington) on the right and No. 24 (ex-Darwen) in the shed. *D.W.K. Jones*

Rhos Depot on the last day of public service with No. 24 (ex-Darwen), No. 5 (ex-Accrington), No. 13 (ex-Bournemouth) and original No. 20 on show. *Vic Bradley*

partitioned-off to provide a smokers' compartment, hence the manufacturer's model name: the 'Preston Patent Semi Convertible Motor Car'. (The basic car could be supplied entirely or partially open or closed as desired by the operator.) Transverse seating in the saloon was for 23, giving a total capacity of 27 passengers. Main dimensions were as follows:

Length of body: over corner posts	20 ft 11 in.
Length of body: over platforms	30 ft 1 in.
Length overall	31 ft 1 in.
Width: over pillars	6 ft 3 in.
Width: over roof	6 ft 6 in.
Height: clear inside at centre	7 ft 10 in.
Height: from rail to trolley base	10 ft 11 in.

Running gear consisted of a four-wheel radial Warner truck of 10-foot wheelbase and equipped with rheostatic and manually-operated brakes. In 1927 all four cars were updated with the fitting of Peckham P35 trucks from Brush, new BTH control equipment and the addition of magnetic brakes.

The whole batch was withdrawn at the same time – winter 1936 following the arrival of the ex-Bournemouth cars (see below) – and stored in the open next to Rhos Depot until 1941 when the trucks were removed and sold to the Leeds Corporation Transport Department where they were used under enclosed double-deck cars Nos. 104, 108, 110 and 433 after regauging to 4 ft 8½ in. The bodies were subsequently disposed of – two of them going to an army camp at Rhyl and two to a similar establishment nearby at Bodelwyddan; their subsequent fate is unrecorded – presumably they simply rotted away.

ORIGINAL CARS NOS. 19–22

The final four cars ordered for the tramway as new came in 1920 from the English Electric Co. Ltd of Preston. These were identical completely open toastrack cars fitted with two English Electric (Mountain & Gibson pattern) equal-wheel bogie trucks. Each truck was powered by a BTH GE149 motor; control was by B18 DD controllers with hand wheel and magnetic braking systems. The lifeguards were of a fixed pattern somewhat reminiscent of railway cowcatchers. Seating was for 60 on lift-over bench seats with seven full-width ones at each end and one half-width one each side of the central trolley standard; the full-width seats held four passengers each and the half-width seats two.

In 1936, with the renumbering of Nos. 6, 10, 11 and 14 (see previous section), toastrack No. 19 was temporarily renumbered 23 until the original No. 10 (now renumbered 19) was scrapped (or at least officially withdrawn) the following year. In 1954 Nos. 19 and 20 were fitted with K4 controllers obtained ex-Sunderland and all four cars were scrapped two years later after the closure of the line though several of the seats are still in Wales, surviving as station benches on the Fairbourne railway in Gwynedd.

Original cars Nos. 17 and 18 at the Rhos depot in 1952.   *H.L. Runnett*

No. 19 at the depot showing the seating arrangement well.   *Peter Johnson Collection*

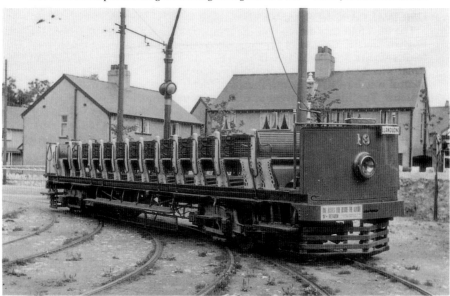

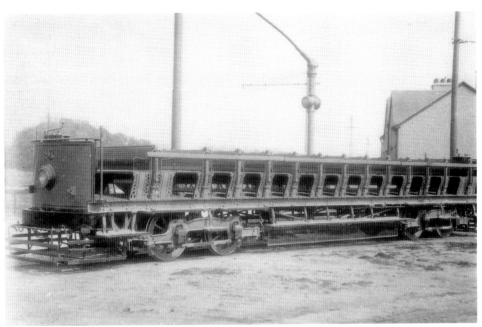

Sister toastrack No. 20 just after delivery and now mounted on its bogies.

Courtesy LCBER Society

Car No. 20 at Llandudno West Shore terminus on 7th September, 1955.

Peter Johnson Collection

Toastrack (No. 21) outside the depot on 21st May, 1951 with footboards in the boarding position. *D.W.K. Jones*

Toastrack No. 21 at the West Shore on 21st May, 1951 on the Light Railway Transport League special. *D.W.K. Jones*

Open toastrack No. 22 in Conway Road after track-doubling. Note the folding boarding steps on the car. *Photographer unknown; Author's Collection*

Works car No. 23 (formerly Bournemouth No. 55) outside the car sheds. *D.W.K. Jones*

No. 1 (ex-Accrington) about to make a run at the 1 in 11½ ascent of Penrhyn Hill in 1937.   *D.W.K. Jones*

No. 1 (ex-Accrington) starting off from the West Shore, 9th June, 1938.   *D.W.K. Jones*

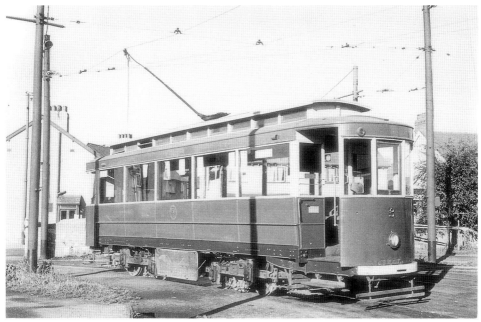

No. 2 (ex-Accrington) in 1938 with new LCBER livery of green and cream.
D.W.K. Jones

No. 3 (ex-Accrington) about to leave the reserved section at the top of Penrhyn Hill, probably during World War II – note the shaded headlamp on the tram and the blanked-off destination indicator on the Crosville Leyland bus.   *D.W.K. Jones*

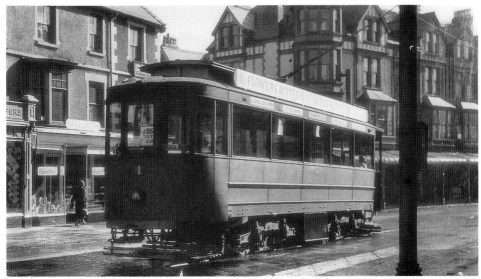

No. 4 (ex-Accrington) at the Colwyn Bay terminus on a very gloomy 17th March, 1956. *Vic Bradley*

The empty interior of No. 5 (ex-Accrington) showing clearly the longitudinal seats and the hanging straps for standing passengers. *D.W.K. Jones*

Car No. 5 (ex-Accrington) seen here at Gloddaeth Street on 11th August, 1955.
John Edgington

No. 5 (ex-Accrington) outside the depot on 9th June, 1938.   *D.W.K. Jones*

No. 17 (the renumbered 14) in the yard on 21st May, 1951; by this date only two of the original 1907 cars survived. *D.W.K. Jones*

The interior saloon of No. 17 (ex-14 of 1907) with the large hand wheel to operate the wheel brakes just visible. *D.W.K. Jones*

SECOND-HAND CARS NOS. 1–5

These five cars were ex-Accrington Corporation single-deckers built by Brush in 1920–22 and purchased by the LCBER in 1932–3 as replacements for the original Nos. 1–5, taking their old numbers. Their Accrington numbers were 28–32 respectively and whilst Nos. 29 and 32 were bought as complete cars, in the case of the other three only the bodies were acquired, these then being mounted on the six better-condition trucks salvaged from the withdrawn Nos. 1–5 to save the expense and trouble of buying and regauging more Accrington trucks than was strictly necessary. (The Accrington system had a 4 ft track gauge.) Those bogies regauged on Nos. 29 and 32 were Brush type C maximum-traction trucks with Dick, Kerr 40 hp 31B motors. Controllers were Dick, Kerr DB1 K3 type.

The car bodies were of the closed saloon pattern with one entrance on each vestibuled end platform; the single trolley was mounted centrally on the monitor roof. Accommodation for 40 passengers was on two longitudinal wooden benches and both hand wheel and magnetic brakes were fitted.

During their new life at Llandudno the cars were subjected to several minor alterations, beginning with the immediate removal of their destination indicator boxes and roof-mounted headlights; the latter were replaced with ones from the original 1907 cars fitted in the standard LCBER position in the centre of the dashes. By 1936 their Accrington red and cream livery had been replaced by the green and cream of Llandudno; two years later the original bench seats were removed and rattan ones from the withdrawn 1907 cars fitted in their place. In 1952–3 all five cars were equipped with self-aligning trolley-heads bought as spares from Birmingham and – a touch of modern comfort – with Dunlopillo seat cushions from the same source. No. 5 also had a change of motors, the new ones coming from the ex-Bournemouth cars (see below).

All five cars survived until the closure.

It should be noted here that the LCBER's car renumbering policy was not as straightforward as might so far appear. The usual tramway practice in such situations was either to allocate second-hand purchases new numbers at the end of the existing fleet list if they simply enlarged it or, if they were intended as replacement vehicles, to give them the numbers of the withdrawn cars. In the case of the LCBER a hybrid policy was formulated whereby the first five second-hand vehicles took the numbers of the five cars they replaced (i.e. 1–5) but the next ten then extended *that* list (i.e. 6, 7 etc) regardless of whether or not the original cars of those numbers had been withdrawn. If they had not, then the *original* cars were renumbered at the end of this new list as detailed above. With the arrival of the last two second-hand cars, this confusing policy was abandoned and they were allocated numbers at the end of the *original* fleet list.

SECOND-HAND CARS NOS. 6–15

The second batch of second-hand cars was acquired from Bournemouth Corporation in 1936 and was a rather mixed lot in all, comprising ten

Car No. 6 (ex-Bournemouth) seen here at West Shore terminus on 11th August, 1955.
John Edgington

No. 6 at Colwyn Bay on 11th August, 1955.   John Edgington

Car No. 7 (ex-Bournemouth) at West Shore terminus on 27th October, 1940.
Peter Johnson Collection

Car No. 7 in Abergele Road, Colwyn Bay (last stop before the terminus) on 28th May, 1946. *E.C. Haywood*

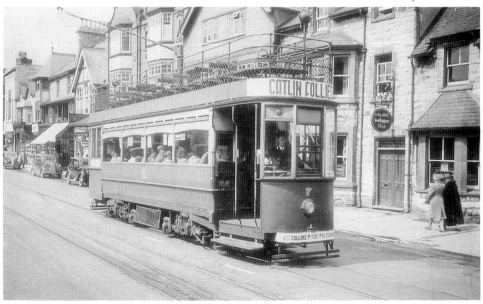

Stopped in the deserted road at Penrhynside on 7th September, 1955, No. 8 (ex-Bournemouth) takes on some additional passengers.   *Peter Johnson Collection*

The final Colwyn Bay terminus on 20th November, 1955 with No. 8 awaiting passengers.   *D.W.K. Jones*

No. 9 (ex-Bournemouth) leaving the reserved Bodafon Fields section shortly after World War II to cross Nant-y-Gamar Road; note the tiny waiting room for passengers on the right. *D.W.K. Jones*

Mostyn Street on 11th August, 1955 with car No. 9 trundling along. *John Edgington*

Viewed from a toastrack car, No. 10 arrives at Rhos on Sea on 11th August, 1955.
John Edgington

No. 11 (ex-Bournemouth) awaiting passengers at the West Shore terminus, 17th March, 1956; behind the houses can be seen the southern slopes of the Great Orme.
Vic Bradley

No. 11 (ex-Bournemouth) undergoing running brake repairs outside the depot on the very last day of public service (21st March, 1956). On the right is the shape of things to come on the morrow. *Vic Bradley*

No. 12 (ex-Bournemouth) at the West Shore terminus. *D.W.K. Jones*

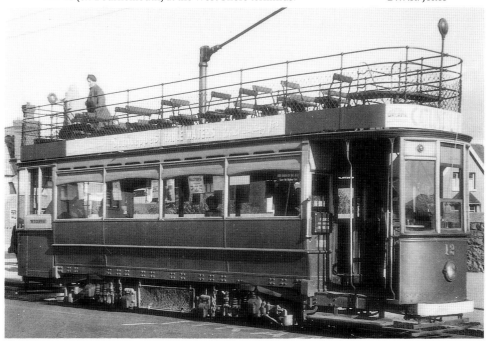

The corner of Gloddaeth Street and Mostyn Street with car No. 13 screeching to a halt. Note the Woolworth 'house style' in August 1955.

John Edgington

A good front view of No. 13; the lower part of the vehicle seems to have had a few encounters with obstructions!

Peter Johnson

No. 14 (ex-Bournemouth) loading in Penrhyn Avenue on the last day of public service.   *Vic Bradley*

No. 14 at the top of Penrhyn Hill.   *D.W.K. Jones*

A busy moment at Hooson's Corner with Nos. 2 and 5 (ex-Accrington) being passed by
No. 15 (ex-Bournemouth).   *D.W.K. Jones*

A cold, damp day in March 1951 with No. 15 and No. 18 passing at Hooson's Corner.
Peter Johnson Collection

passenger cars and one works car (see below); the passenger cars were of two separate designs though all were standard open-top, double-deck vehicles. The first design was represented by No. 6 (Bournemouth 85), built by United Electric in 1914. It had elliptically-shaped end platforms with vestibules that dated from 1920. The bogies were Brill 22E maximum-traction trucks with a Westinghouse 226N motor in each, giving a total of 80 hp. Other electrical equipment was also by Westinghouse while the lifeguards were by Hudson-Browning. Three braking systems were fitted: hand wheel, magnetic and hand track. After arriving at Llandudno the old motors were replaced with the LCBER's favourite BTH GE249s, these in turn being replaced in 1953 by two of the batch of Dick, Kerr type 30B 40 hp motors obtained from Birmingham that year along with their accompanying gears, wheels and axles. This car remained in service to the closure and, as described in Chapter 8, has by good fortune been preserved.

The second design was made up of two groups in terms of age. All were from Brush, the older group being built in 1921 and numbered (Bourne-mouth numbers in brackets): 9 (108), 10 (103), 11 (95) and 13 (112). They were similar to No. 6 in design but with slightly longer semi-circular vestibuled end platforms. Trucks were again Brill 22Es but with BTH B49 motors and B49CC controllers. Again the motors developed 40 hp, the same as their BTH GE249 replacements. Braking systems were the same as those on No. 6; in 1953 all were fitted with ex-Birmingham motors, gears and wheelsets too. Nos. 9 and 10 were scrapped in January 1956 while Nos. 11 and 13 survived until the closure in March.

The younger group comprised five cars, built 1924-6 and numbered (Bournemouth numbers in brackets): 7 (115), 8 (116), 12 (128), 14 (121) and 15 (114). Trucks were Brill 22Es with Metrovick 40 hp motors and con-trollers. Upon arrival GE249 motors were fitted and in 1954 Nos. 8, 12 and 15 were re-equipped in a similar manner to Nos. 6, 9, 10, 11 and 13. No. 7 held the dubious honour of being Bournemouth's 'last car' while No. 8 was of course later awarded a similar distinction on the LCBER. All five survived until the closure then went the way of the rest for scrapping.

More detailed dimensions of these cars are given below:

	No. 6	Nos. 7–15
Wheelbase: bogie	4 ft 0 in.	4 ft 0 in.
Wheelbase: total	20 ft 0 in.	20 ft 0 in.
Length: over body	23 ft 6 in.	23 ft 6 in.
Length: overall	35 ft 6 in.	36 ft 6 in.
Width	6 ft 4 in.	6 ft 4 in.
Seating: upper deck	32	38
Seating: lower deck	30	30

SECOND-HAND CARS NOS. 23 AND 24

The last two cars acquired by the LCBER were ex-Darwen Nos. 24 and 23, renumbered 23 and 24 respectively at Llandudno. (Just why these numbers were reversed is a mystery.) They were modern, enclosed, double-deck trams built in 1936 by English Electric as a reduced-width version of a

No. 23 (ex-Darwen) on shuttle service at the (final) Colwyn Bay terminus.

Lens of Sutton

No. 24 (ex-Darwen) on the interlaced track in Colwyn Bay, May 1951.   *D.W.K. Jones*

standard gauge design developed 1933–5 for Blackpool's tramways (one variant being the famous 'Balloons'). At Darwen their size and streamlined bodywork earned them the nickname of 'Queens' as a shortened form of 'Queen Mary's' (the liner of that name having been launched in 1934). Entry was via an entrance on each side with a central staircase to the upper deck; the single trolley was centrally mounted on the roof. The pair arrived at Llandudno in 1946 but their testing over the tramway was delayed until late 1947 as their maximum-traction bogie trucks had been sent to Burton-on-Trent for regauging from 4 ft. Each car was powered by two 57 hp English Electric motors and was equipped with English Electric/Dick, Kerr K33 type controllers. Other modern refinements were air hooters and air brakes.

At Llandudno the cars were felt to be underpowered, a defect that possibly dated back to June 1936 when, during trials at Darwen, No. 23 (LCBER No. 24) derailed under a low bridge and was subsequently modified with, it is believed, smaller wheels. (This would also help account for the fact that on the LCBER rolling on poor track caused the cars to ground their bodywork.)

Each lower saloon held 12 passengers on transverse seats (upholstered in green, as for Blackpool, even when sporting Darwen's red and cream livery) whilst the narrower upper saloon held 32 on 2 and 1 transverse seats (the centre aisle changed sides at the top of the stairs). Six destination blinds were fitted: two side by side over the cab front windows at each end and one over each entrance. It was intended that they should form a basis of a whole new fleet at Darwen but they were not a success – they rolled a lot on poor track there as well – and by March 1945 both were out of service; it seems clear now that the standard gauge design had not been modified sufficiently – for reasons of economy – to suit a narrower gauge system. By the end of that year however both had been overhauled, presumably with a view to their sale, and in January 1946 the LCBER put in a firm offer of £400 each for them. On 19th August that year No. 23 left Lancashire by road for Wales, followed four days later by No. 24; the Darwen system closed on 5th October.

As described above in Chapter 6, these two cars were prohibited by the Ministry of Transport from working the more exposed stretches of the tramway, their 4 ft gauge-designed closed superstructure being deemed to make them vulnerable to over-turning in high winds. Instead, they were put on shuttle services in Llandudno and Colwyn Bay in 1948, though No. 23 was withdrawn from its Llandudno working after only a year as the condition of sections of the track there was so bad that it was having a damaging effect upon the car; this was despite the service being reduced to cover just Mostyn Street and Mostyn Broadway. It seems they were liked by their new drivers – who nicknamed them 'Spivs' – but not by many of their passengers, some of whom complained of sea-sickness induced by the cars' propensity to roll and sway. Although both were officially withdrawn in 1954, they were actually the last cars to be scrapped in 1956 after the closure of the line as the company entertained hopes of being able to sell them (but to whom?).

A good side-on view of one of the ex-Darwen cars, its low ground clearance evident even when unladen. *Lens of Sutton*

The lower saloon interior of No. 24, showing the centre entrance and stairs.
D.W.K. Jones

More detailed dimensions are given below:

Length overall	35 ft 6 in.
Width	6 ft 7½ in.
Height: rail to trolley plank	14 ft 8 in.
Wheelbase	4 ft 6 in.

LIVERY

Basic livery for the original cars was maroon below the waist and cream above, fully lined-out in gold. Nos. 1–14 had the legend 'LLANDUDNO & COLWYN BAY' in gold in the centre of the waist panels on each side whilst the car number was painted in gold above the electric headlight in the centre of each dash. Nos. 15–18 carried the legend 'LLANDUDNO & COLWYN BAY ELECTRIC RAILWAY LIMITED' along the whole length of the rocker panel on each side while the car number, again in gold, was repeated on both sides of the dash headlights. In the centre of each waist panel was a coat of arms design.

During World War I Nos. 1–14 were painted battleship grey as a temporary measure but some cars continued to sport this colour until they were withdrawn or repainted in the new official livery of green and cream in 1933 (as were the other original cars). At the same time official crests (different from the earlier design) were added to the sides of the closed trams.

All the second-hand cars were, sooner or later, repainted in the official 1933 livery which was basically green panels, cream framing, dark orange roofs, dark brown underframes, red oxide trucks and lifeguards and black fenders. Gold numbers were carried above the headlight in the centre of each dash with the company crest displayed on each side of the body.

INDICATORS

The original Nos. 1–14 were equipped, as delivered, with destination boards hung at the bottom of the windows in the centre of each side and at each end of the car. Later, in line with the company's standard policy, roof boards were added on each side giving details of the complete route travelled. Those cars that had one side entrance enclosed on each end platform had the front destination boxes on the roof at each end, but these were later replaced by standard route boards on each side and a metal destination sign hung in the nearside front window. The toastracks simply hung one of these destination signs on the front dash.

The second-hand cars purchased before World War II were adapted in line with the above policy; during the war years all these signs and boards disappeared though the signs were later reinstated. It was not until the tramway's final years that any other indicators were used: black-printed yellow paper strips above the windows of the closed cars or, in the case of the toastracks, stuck on the lower off-side of the dashes. In the case of cars Nos. 23 and 24 a slightly different arrangement was used: destination boards above the cab windows giving (for No. 23) the Llandudno terminal points and (for No. 24) the Colwyn Bay ones.

Works car No. 23 – sporting its stairs to nowhere – in 1938 with car No. 2 (ex-Accrington) in new LCBER livery behind. *D.W.K. Jones*

No. 24 outside the depot on 21st May, 1951. *D.W.K. Jones*

One of the Brill maximum traction trucks as fitted to car No. 6 (ex-Bournemouth).
D.W.K. Jones

A close-up view of a Mountain & Gibson truck from one of the 1907 cars removed for servicing in the depot, sometime during the 1920s. *Courtesy LCBER Society*

Another view of a Mountain & Gibson equal-wheel truck, this time under 1907 car
No. 17 (formerly 14). *D.W.K. Jones*

One of the Brush maximum traction trucks as fitted to car No. 2 (ex-Accrington).
D.W.K. Jones

The driver's controls of one of the ex-Bournemouth cars (No. 8) showing the large controller handle on the left (in 'off' position), the small forward-reverse-neutral key and the track brake wheel topped by the wheel brake handle.   *D.W.K. Jones*

The crew of No. 8 enjoy a brief stop-over at the West Shore in November 1955. Note the conductor's heavy clothing – especially useful on the top deck in a Welsh winter!
D.W.K. Jones

WORKS CARS

During its life the LCBER possessed two powered works cars. The first was originally built by Brush in 1901 for the Taunton & West Somerset Electric Railways & Tramways Co. Ltd (later the Taunton Electric Traction Co. Ltd). It was an open-top, double-deck, four-wheeled passenger car with a 6 ft 6 in. wheelbase and magnetic brakes; the handbrakes were mounted outside the shallow dashes and the downward-pointing headlamp at each end was carried on the upper-deck sheeting. In 1905, with the reconstruction of the Taunton system, it was sold (along with the other five original cars) to the newly-electrified Leamington & Warwick Tramways. Here it was numbered (probably) 11 – its Taunton number is unknown – and converted into a scrubber car. In 1930 it moved again (the Balfour, Beatty-owned Leamington line closed that August), this time to Llandudno where it remained in use for six years before becoming, less running gear, a stores shed. (Presumably before 1930 one of the passenger cars would have been pressed into service whenever a works vehicle was needed.)

The line's second works car was obtained in 1936 to replace the one described above and it possessed a similarly eventful history. It had also begun life in 1901, this time as a G.F. Milnes product for the Poole & District Electric Traction Co. (P&DET) as double-deck, open-top, four-wheeled passenger car No. 1 on a Brill 21E truck. In 1905 it was acquired, along with the rest of the P&DET, by Bournemouth Corporation Tramways and renumbered 55. Wheelbase was 6 ft, as was its width; length was 16 ft over the body and 27 ft 7 in. overall. Controllers were BTH B18s and the motors G58s from the same firm; the lifeguards were by Tidswell. In 1921, whilst still at Bournemouth, No. 55 was converted into a rail-grinder and the top deck removed – although a rather peculiar visual effect resulted from the fact that neither staircase was so treated! It came to Llandudno with the other Bournemouth cars purchased in 1936 and was given a plain grey livery and the number 23. In 1947, after the arrival of the ex-Darwen cars, it was renumbered 23A.

In addition to these two cars (both of which ran on 3 ft 6 in. gauge lines throughout their lives) the LCBER also operated at least four non-powered items of rolling stock, including a welding unit and a small trailer bogie for carrying rails which was obtained from Coventry Corporation in 1941; these two essential maintenance vehicles were simply towed to wherever needed by a works car and then positioned manually. There were, in addition, at least two four-wheeled trucks – possibly dating from the construction of the line – which were used to carry sand for the trams back to the depot whilst being pushed or pulled by one of the powered cars. In the early years this sand was collected from the West Shore; in later years it came from Penrhyn Bay. When not in use the trucks were kept in a siding on Penrhyn Hill.

The tramway's other vital maintenance vehicle was its road-going tower wagon for servicing the overhead. It is thought the LCBER operated two during its lifetime, a Fordson truck (registration number EUN 148) purchased new in 1948 replacing the original wooden, horse-drawn one.

Appendix One
Fleet List

No.	Built	Builder	Type	Withdrawn	Remarks
Original stock: the closed single-deckers					
1	1907	MRC&W	8wb	1932/3	
2	,,	,,	,,	,,	
3	,,	,,	,,	,,	
4	,,	,,	,,	,,	
5	,,	,,	,,	,,	
6	,,	,,	,,	1945	Renumbered 16 in 1936
7	,,	,,	,,	1936	
8	,,	,,	,,	,,	
9	,,	,,	,,	,,	
10	,,	,,	,,	1937	Renumbered 19 in 1936
11	,,	,,	,,	1956	Renumbered 18 in 1936
12	,,	,,	,,	1936	
13	,,	,,	,,	,,	
14	,,	,,	,,	1956	Renumbered 17 in 1936
15	1909	UEC	4wt	1936	Broken-up 1941
16	,,	,,	,,	,,	,,
17	,,	,,	,,	,,	,,
18	,,	,,	,,	,,	,,
Original stock: the toastracks					
19	1920	EE	8wb	1956	Briefly renumbered 23 in 1936
20	,,	,,	,,	,,	
21	,,	,,	,,	,,	
22	,,	,,	,,	,,	
Second-hand stock: the closed single-deckers acquired 1932/3					
1	1920–2	Brush	8wb	1956	Ex-Accrington 28
2	,,	,,	,,	,,	Ex-Accrington 29
3	,,	,,	,,	,,	Ex-Accrington 30
4	,,	,,	,,	,,	Ex-Accrington 31
5	,,	,,	,,	,,	Ex-Accrington 32
Second-hand stock: the open-top double-deckers acquired 1936					
6	1914	UEC	8wb	1956	Ex-Bournemouth 85; preserved
7	1924–6	Brush	,,	,,	Ex-Bournemouth 115
8	,,	,,	,,	,,	Ex-Bournemouth 116
9	1921	,,	,,	,,	Ex-Bournemouth 108
10	,,	,,	,,	,,	Ex-Bournemouth 103
11	,,	,,	,,	,,	Ex-Bournemouth 95
12	1924–6	,,	,,	,,	Ex-Bournemouth 128
13	1921	,,	,,	,,	Ex-Bournemouth 112
14	1924–6	,,	,,	,,	Ex-Bournemouth 121
15	,,	,,	,,	,,	Ex-Bournemouth 114

Second-hand stock: the closed double-deckers acquired 1946

| 23 | 1936 | EE | 8wb | 1954 | Ex-Darwen 24; cut-up 1956 |
| 24 | ,, | ,, | ,, | ,, | Ex-Darwen 23; cut-up 1956 |

Powered works cars

| — | 1901 | Brush | 4wt | 1936 | Scrubber car acquired ex-Leamington & Warwick; formerly Taunton open-top double-decker |
| 23 | ,, | Milnes | ,, | 1956 | Rail-grinder acquired 1936 ex-Bournemouth; formerly Poole open-top double-decker. Re-numbered 23A in 1947. |

No. 23 holding up the traffic between Rhos on Sea and Colwyn Bay, in June 1952.
H.L. Runnett

Rhos Depot with the tramway's horse-
drawn tower wagon in the foreground
and a toastrack inside the original shed.
(A second shed was built on this side to
accommodate the fleet enlargement of
the 1930s.)   *Courtesy LCBER Society*

The former car sheds, 1992.
                    M. Donnison

The refurbished LCBER office building
beside the former car sheds, 1992.
                    M. Donnison

Looking towards the West Shore, 1992; little has changed since the 1920s except the size of the trees – and the traffic.   *M. Donnison*

The former reserved section through Bodafon Fields, 1992, with Nant-y-Gamar Road in the foreground and the Little Orme in the distance.   *Author*

The former toll road on an overcast day in late 1992 with the new sea wall on the left and the entrance to the Golf Club on the right.   *Author*

Appendix Two
Fleet List of the Buses

Fleet No.   Reg. No.   Built   Body   Withdrawn   Remarks

Driver training vehicle bought 1955 ex-East Kent
(Leyland Titan TD5 chassis)

–	AJG 26	1938	Park Royal	1956	

Spares vehicle bought 1956 ex-Southdown
(Guy Arab 5LW chassis)

–	GUF 175	1945	Weymann	–	

Original service vehicles bought 1956 ex-Newcastle
(Daimler CO5G chassis)

1	HTN 231	1939	Northern Coach Builders	1961	Converted to open-top 1956
2	HTN 233	,,	,,	,,	

Original service vehicles bought 1956 ex-Southdown
(Guy Arab 5LW chassis)

3	GUF 128	1945	Northern Counties	1957	
4	GUF 133	,,	,,	1959	
5	GUF 155	,,	,,	1957.	Rebuilt as break-down tender
6	GUF 165	,,	,,	1959	
7	GUF 177	,,	Weymann	1961	
8	GUF 183	,,	,,	,,	
9	GUF 387	,,	,,	,,	
10	GUF 388	,,	,,	,,	
11	GUF 391	1946	,,	,,	
12	GUF 393	,,	,,	,,	
13	GUF 398	,,	Park Royal	,,	

Replacement service vehicle bought 1957 ex-Southdown
(Guy Arab 5LW chassis)

3	GUF 159	1945	Northern Counties	1961	Converted to open-top 1960

Replacement service vehicles bought 1959 ex-East Kent
(Guy Arab 5LW chassis)

4	BJG 355	1944	Park Royal	1961	
6	BJG 356	,,	,,	,,	

Ex-Southdown GUF 128 waiting to take over from tramcar No. 6 (ex-Bournemouth) in May 1956.   *D.W.K. Jones*

No. 6 and ex-East Kent Leyland AJG 26 successor – used for driver training – outside the depot during the tramway's final days.   *D.W.K. Jones*

Appendix Three
Relics

The story of the LCBER would not be complete without mention of the connections it has with a tramway which did not even exist when the Llandudno line closed. This is the Seaton Tramway on the south coast of Devon, the beginnings of which can be found in a portable 15 in. gauge line constructed by Mr C.W. Lane, a New Barnet engineer and manufacturer of battery-electric delivery vehicles. After three years' operation at fêtes and the like (including trials in 1951 on a semi-permanent line at St Leonards on the south coast) a permanent site was sought and in 1952 it opened as the ¼ mile Voryd Park miniature tramway in Rhyl. The first of the line's two original cars was a one-third scale model of LCBER No. 23 with a centre entrance and straight staircase for practical reasons; even so, accommodation on the two decks was somewhat cramped! (The other car – No. 225 – was a model of a Blackpool prototype.)

In 1954 the line was moved by its operator – now known as Modern Electric Tramways Ltd – to a bigger site at Eastbourne and rebuilt to a 2 ft gauge; No. 23 was consequently sold. In 1969 this line too closed and the tramway moved to occupy the southern portion of the old London & South Western Railway branch from Seaton Junction to Seaton, opening in 1970 on yet another new gauge of 2 ft 9 in. After the line went to Eastbourne (and of course again at Seaton) the wider gauge(s) made it possible for new trams to be constructed utilising actual equipment obtained from scrapped 'full-size' cars. Thus Eastbourne cars Nos. 2, 4, 6, 7 and 12 incorporated (together with parts from other systems' trams) the following items:

No. 2 (1963 Eastbourne): parts of LCBER cars used in the construction of bulk-heads and sliding doors.

No. 4 (1961 Eastbourne): motorman's valves, air whistles, controllers and circuit-breakers from the LCBER's ex-Darwen cars.

No. 6 (1953 New Barnet; rebuilt 1956 and 1961): top deck seats and scroll work from LCBER No. 8 (ex-Bournemouth); headlamps, gongs, signal-bells and circuit-breakers from various other LCBER cars.

No. 7 (1958 New Barnet): top deck seats from the LCBER's ex-Bournemouth cars; headlamps, gongs, signal-bells, circuit-breakers and controllers from LCBER No. 3 (ex-Accrington).

No. 12 (1966 Eastbourne): the other two controllers from the LCBER's ex-Darwen cars.

The notice boards at the Rhos end of the toll road. Note the officially-correct reference to 'light railway' rather than 'tramway'.   *D.W.K. Jones*

Trams no more: the pair of surviving destination boards now on show in the National Tramway Museum, Crich.   *M. Donnison*

Appendix Four
Other Tramway Proposals

The LCBER was not of course the only tramway to be built in Llandudno: from 1902 onwards the Great Orme Tramway (GOT) has filled its specialised role of taking visitors (and residents) up the southern slopes of the Great Orme. The history of this cable tramway has been covered comprehensively elsewhere and although no other tramways were constructed in either Llandudno or Colwyn Bay, three proposals deserve mention. The most ambitious of these, reported in the local press in September 1903, was for an electric light railway to link West Kirby on the Wirral with Rhyl, Colwyn Bay and Llandudno. Perhaps not surprisingly, since it would have entailed the construction of a bridge (or causeway and bridge) at least four miles long across the Dee estuary, nothing more was heard of this scheme.

The second proposal was for a far less ambitious but equally spectacular line. In 1879 a private toll road had been constructed around the entire headland of the Great Orme for those visitors daring enough to walk or ride from east to west along a road that clung to the very side of the rockface. Constructed at a cost of £14,000 the Marine Drive – as it was named – was 4 miles 130 yards in length (although the distance between entrance and exit across the peninsular was less than 1½ miles) and proved such a success that in 1897 it was purchased by Llandudno UDC.

Even before the road had been opened fully though suggestions were being made to replace it with a tramway. One such proposal came from the writer of a letter to the *Caernarvon & Denbigh Herald* of 21st August, 1875 who claimed that the tram fare would be in the region of only 3d. (1p) compared with the sum of 5s. (25p) charged by the fly drivers who drove people round the Orme. The suggestion though remained just a suggestion for a quarter of a century until, during the protracted birth of the LCBER, Llandudno UDC decided to investigate the matter more fully. The General Purposes Committee submitted a report by the Engineer, Mr E. Paley Stephenson, to the Council in November 1901; the report was a detailed study for what would be known as the Great Orme's Head Marine Drive Tramway. It was to follow the plan of the proposed Llandudno–Colwyn Bay line in that it would be a 3 ft 6 in. gauge electric overhead tramway; on the actual Marine Drive section of the route from the Happy Valley Lodge on the eastern side of the Orme to the Penmorfa Lodge on the west the line was to run 3 ft from the kerb on the landward side of the road whilst on the town side of the Orme two alternative routes were considered. The first was via Abbey Road, West Parade, Conway Crescent, Gloddaeth Street and North Parade; the second was via Abbey Road, Tudnor Street, Church Walks (later the terminus for the GOT) and North Parade. The first route was the preferred one of the two as a possible agreement could then be reached with the Llandudno & Colwyn Bay promoters for common running over this section. The second route, on the other hand, would be the more costly one to build and operate and would also raise more opposition from residents.

Construction of the line would have entailed the removal of about 1,350 cubic yards of rock from the Drive as the road was discovered by Stephenson to be narrower than the statutory 16 ft in several places. The cost of construction was estimated at £34,000 for the first route and £35,000 for the second. A 15 minute service was envisaged running in an anti-clockwise direction around the headland with both open and closed cars and a fare of 6d. (2½p).

It is tempting to speculate as to whether or not the tramway would still be with us today if it had been built – but it was not, killed as the proposal was by the reluctance of the Council to begin a new tramway venture when it might well be called upon to complete the one already on its doorstep, opposition from the Llandudno Pier Co. who foresaw a possible loss of revenue and (one would imagine) similar opposition from the promoters of the GOT. Only one comparable line was ever built in the British Isles: that on the Douglas Head Marine Drive in the Isle of Man – coincidentally just a summer steamer's day trip away from Llandudno. Opened in 1896, its construction doubtless played some part in the minds of the Llandudno councillors but since it failed to re-open after World War II it is realistic to assume that its Welsh counterpart, like so many other railways and tramways, might well have become a fellow casualty.

The third proposal was for a much shorter line altogether: along the seashore by the Parade from opposite St George's Hospital at its northern end as far as the Little Orme (a distance of about 1½ miles). The idea was put to the local Board in November 1892 but was turned down. Curiously, although the line was to be worked by electricity, it was to be laid actually on the beach next to the Parade, not on the roadway itself. Presumably the intention was that such a siting of the line would result in no inconvenience to the resort's promenaders, thus making the proposal more attractive; the ploy however was an unsuccessful one, as was the promoters' promise to install electric lighting on the Parade if permission for the tramway were to be granted.

Bibliography

Anderson, R.C. *A History of Crosville Motor Services*, David & Charles, 1981.

Anderson, R.C. *A History of the Llandudno & Colwyn Bay Electric Railway Limited*, Quail Map Co., Exeter, 1968.

Crosland-Taylor, W.J. *Crosville: The Sowing and the Harvest*, Littlebury Bros, Liverpool, 1948; 2nd edition Transport Publishing Co., 1987.

Lawson, R. & Morris, G.C.J. *The Llandudno & Colwyn Bay Electric Railway*, Light Railway Transport League, 1956.

Martin, Brian P. (editor): *Trams . . . a nostalgic look back*, Llandudno Tramway Society.

Price, Geoff: *Trams leave here for Llandudno and Colwyn Bay*, Pride Books, Carnforth, 1983.

Smith, Peter M. *Llandudno and Colwyn Bay Electric Railway in the 1920s*, Llandudno & Colwyn Bay Electric Railway Society.

Tucker, N. *Colwyn Bay: its origin and growth*, Colwyn Bay Borough Council, 1953.

Turner, Keith: *North Wales Tramways*, David & Charles, 1979.

Other printed sources consulted include appropriate trade directories and journals, transport history journals, local newspapers, relevant statutory instruments, reports of the Light Railway Commissioners, official returns, Ordnance Survey maps, timetables and sundry other items of ephemeral material relating to the background, setting and history of the LCBER.